SABINA REIGNS

A NOVEL

LORRAINE BARTLETT

❀ Created with Vellum

ACKNOWLEDGMENTS

My thanks for Mary Kennedy Psy. D, and Gayle Trent for their brainstorming, and Shirley Hailstock for her always-valuable input and support.

Thank you to members of the Lorraine Train: Mary Ann Borer, Debbie Lyon, and Pam Priest. You ladies rock!

CAST OF CHARACTERS

SABINA REIGNS: (her maiden name); mother, soon-to-be ex-wife, and frustrated entrepreneur

JONATHAN MILLER: Sabina's husband of twenty years, partner in a law firm

JULIE BAXTER: a caterer, divorced single mom, and Sabina's best friend

MARISA MILLER: Sabina's college-age daughter

ZOEY BAXTER: Julie's pregnant teen daughter

TODD FOREMAN: purports to be Sabina's new assistant; formerly worked for Charles Patterson, but left under suspicious circumstances

STEVE MEADE: Sabina's contractor

COURTNEY SULLIVAN: Jonathan's mistress and mother of his love child

CHARLES PATTERSON: owner of the largest interior design firm in the area

GEORGIA WILCOX: curator of the Parkview Manor and in charge of its renovation

"*D*ivorcing? You and Jonathan?" Sabina Reigns Miller's best friend, Julie Baxter, wailed, her voice distorted by the phone's tiny speaker. "Oh, honey, why didn't you call me sooner?" Julie had been Sabina's best friend since third grade. They'd weathered good times and bad, including Julie's daughter trouble, and Sabina's somewhat strained relationship with her own daughter; Julie's divorce, and now Sabina's. No matter what crisis either of them faced, they had always depended on each other as a cheering squad, a source of tough love, or a shoulder to cry on. This was no different.

"I was going to—but I knew you had catering jobs up the wazoo for the last couple of weeks. Besides, I needed to get a lot done in a short span of time," Sabina said and plopped onto the comforter that covered the queen size bed.

"Like what?"

"I wasn't about to spend another night with that stinking serial cheater. First, I moved into the guest room. But more importantly, I've been invited to bid on a big redecoration project. I've already started work on my presentation."

Julie smacked her lips, reminding Sabina of some mid-forties

Jersey mom. "You're holding up too well," Julie sang. "When Larry left me, I was devastated."

Sabina snorted. "Jonathan's not miserable, he's got a much younger version of me now—so, why should I be bummed? And sorting through my clothes and things has been good therapy. I've got my own attorney and the settlement details are already being hammered out. They say possession is nine-tenths of the law, and I wasn't about to leave the house until I had an idea of what I could expect."

"Good for you," Julie cheered.

As Sabina talked, she stared down at a pile of clothes she was going through, unsure if she was even going to bother taking them. They all had some sort of emotional memory involving Jonathan. A specially bought anniversary dress, gifts, and outfits from more frivolous occasions like vacations and holidays. Sabina couldn't help but shake her head at the way she, and every other human, attached memories to the strangest things.

Shrugging, she started filling a bag. "Jonathan might be a philanderer, but so far he's been fair. Or maybe he's just desperate to get me out—fast. He agreed to advance me a bundle to 'start a new life.' We're negotiating for the furniture I'll take, and what he wants to keep. It's all been very civilized."

"But where will you go?" Julie asked.

"An apartment, for now." Sabina didn't have the time or the energy to look for a house, although she already knew exactly what she wanted—an old farmhouse outside of Rochester. She wanted to look out on pasture or woods, a place far enough out that she could see the stars clearly at night. A place of peace and quiet, and maybe even solitude. A haven from the city, but not so far out that the commute was unreasonable. Finding her slice of paradise would take a while. And she was willing to wait.

"I don't even care where I live for the time being. I have more important matters to think about."

Julie huffed. "Isn't getting a divorce enough?"

"I've had my DBA for years. Now I'm finally going to officially start my own business." Sabina stopped and grinned, forgetting she hadn't yet told Julie. Well, they'd spoken about it for years—but she hadn't told her it was now going to be a reality.

Julie sounded almost sad. "Good grief, you *are* moving on."

"I called a real estate agent to find me an apartment *and* a retail space."

"Don't you think you're rushing into things?" For some reason, even considering all Julie had been through herself, she still sounded far more nervous than Sabina felt about the big change in her life.

"No. I'm not. Life is short, and I've wasted far too much of mine catering to Jonathan. Now, it's my turn." Sabina stood and reached for the frame sitting on top of the dresser, tossing her wedding photo in the wastebasket.

* * *

LATER THAT AFTERNOON, Sabina sat primly in the uncomfortable gray upholstered chair, dressed in her most conservative navy linen suit, matching leather purse, and shoes, feeling like she was going on a job interview—which, she guessed she was. She brushed at her strawberry-blonde bangs and waited expectantly for the good news, waited as Jason Stone, the loan officer, shuffled through a pile of papers on his desk. Finally, he took off his glasses and tapped them on his open palm.

"I'm sorry, Ms. Reigns, but Mr. Miller has decided not to co-sign the loan."

If only the man had whipped out a digital camera right then and there, Sabina was sure he would have captured the hysterical image of her bulging eyes and gaping mouth when she heard the news.

"What?" Sabina yelped. "What?"

Stone squirmed. "Err, it seems he's had a change of heart. If

3

you could find some other friend or relative who'd be willing to—"

Every sound in the room muted and Sabina was left in a whirlwind of thoughts and an expanding rage.

No loan.

She was about to give up her beautiful home and was sitting on orders for thousands of dollars' worth of merchandise to stock her new business venture, all on her soon-to-be ex-husband's promise that he would co-sign a business loan.

Sabina had no real money of her own. Jonathan's insistence that she remain a stay-at-home mom had made sure of that.

She rose from her chair and was about to thank Stone when she reconsidered. Why should she thank another man who was content to keep her from achieving her dreams? Instead, she walked out of the office without even mumbling goodbye. She was too numb to speak. But behind the numbness boiled anger. She'd been brought up never to use four-letter words, but that didn't mean she didn't know them, or how to use them for that matter. At that moment, Sabina wanted to hurl every foul word she could think of straight at Jonathan and watch them simmer like acid on his skin. In that singular moment, she wanted to hurt him in every way she possibly could. She had attempted to keep things civil despite his barbaric showing of hedonism when choosing to stray from their marriage, but that restraint was quickly slipping through her fingers.

Sabina had spent her life living under the thumbs of far too many people—mostly men. Divorce could be devastating, sure, but it could also be freeing, powerful, and filled with motivation for the future. Her entire plan revolved around the idea that she could have a fresh start. And sure, the co-signer would be her ex, but he at least owed her that. After everything he had put her through, he should have been absorbing the cost, instead of co-signing the loan.

Nonetheless, a promise was a promise. Besides, he got something out of it, too. He got silence. *Her silence.* The amount of damning information she had collected on him through the years would easily knock him right on his butt.

Sabina frowned; she didn't have that kind of malice within her. She was already scorned and angered by what Jonathan had done to their marriage, to their future, and to their daughter. So, trading a silence she had already planned on keeping was a no brainer for her.

The silence wasn't for *him* though, it was for their daughter, Marisa. It was a way to keep her from seeing the hurtful truth of how terrible her father was—incapable, really—when it came to loving people. How he had thrown away years of marriage for what felt good at the moment. It was a barrier preventing Marisa from discovering her father's true nature.

Sabina stomped out of the bank and onto the sidewalk, walking swiftly through the crowd of office workers on their lunch hours. She mumbled to herself in anger as her feet slapped the pavement. She was an angry woman, one with purpose and determination. One with a very large, very heavy axe to grind.

"Apparently Jonathan has never heard of the old saying," she grumbled as she turned into the parking garage. "A woman scorned," she huffed loudly, making a high-pitched laughing noise. "The woman scorned is talking to herself in the dang parking garage. That's what she's doing."

She slowed her pace a bit, feeling a stinging sensation beneath the soles of the sensible flats she had slipped on to go to her meeting. Sure, the other woman pranced around in four-inch designer heels. So far, she didn't have battle wounds from pregnancy and childbirth. She was freaking perfect.

Well, that wouldn't last.

The keys slipped from Sabina's hand and fell to the concrete as she approached her car. She leaned her head back and let out a deep sigh, feeling the weight of the situation almost burying her. Reaching down, she picked them up and silently got into her car.

Carefully, she shut the door and gripped the steering wheel. She sat there in complete silence for several moments before shaking herself forward and back, her hair flying everywhere, screaming at the top of her lungs.

When she was finished, she patted down the wild hair and shook her shoulders. Giving herself a firm nod of satisfaction for getting it out of her system for the moment, she glanced over at a guy getting in his car. She didn't know how long he'd been standing there, but from the look of his frozen posture and startled expression, he was likely to have witnessed the entire show.

Sabina laughed nervously and gave him a wave before starting the car and tearing out of there. She knew that was not where she needed to be scaring unsuspecting innocents. Where she needed to be was obvious, and Jonathan wasn't going to like the not-so-surprise visit he was about to receive.

Completely flustered, Sabina reached down and jabbed her finger against the stereo knob. The sound of classic pop hits pumped loudly from the speakers, the soundtrack she had played as she was on her way to the bank just an hour before. She'd felt exhilarated, singing along with the music, feeling as though she was finally freeing herself to chase her dreams.

An hour later, she couldn't turn the happy beats off fast enough. Her fingers strummed against the steering wheel, trying to calm herself. Her phone, vibrating in the center console caught her attention. Without taking her eyes off the road, she rummaged around, finally pulling it out. She hoped for his sake that it wasn't her ex, because there was no restraint in her whatsoever.

She stabbed the accept-call icon and speaker. "Hello?"

"So, are you the happy owner of a big fat check?" Julie asked with glee.

"I am going to rip his arms off, shove them up his ass, and then dance around him shaking a stick like he's being sacrificed to the infidelity Gods," Sabina replied evenly.

There was silence for a moment. "He didn't show up, did he?"

There was that laugh again, shrill, malicious, and hoarse in her throat. "Oh no, of course he didn't show up. I was literally sitting there in front of the loan officer who had to be the one to tell me."

Julie hissed through her teeth, and Sabina could picture her friend wincing. "And where are you going now?"

"Where else would I go? To his office so I can kick his butt," Sabina said.

"Sabina," Julie warned.

Sabina let out a long deep sigh. "Don't worry, I won't resort to physical violence. Not yet anyway. I will, however, march my rear straight in there and demand that he do what he promised. I will no longer stand down in this situation. If he's going to wage war on me, I will defend myself and redeem what is rightly mine."

"Good lord," Julie said and giggled. "You sound like a nobleman whose beloved was just stolen by a ferocious dragon hiding in the mountains. Will you be wearing armor?"

"Mental armor," Sabina replied. "And I know that's not something he ever dons, especially when he doesn't know I'm heading straight for him."

Julie laughed. "I mean, he has to have an idea you're coming though. He knows you have a temper and he knows this is important to you."

"And he's going to know that if he doesn't treat me fairly, I will bring hell down around his shoulders," Sabina added. "He miscalculated if he thinks I'm just playing around with plans to open a business. That I'll sit back and just let him take my marriage, my house, my furniture, and my daughter without a fight. He has royally screwed up this time. Royally."

Julie smacked her lips. "Well, I wish you luck. Don't forget to breathe. And try not to hit the big-shot attorney in front of witnesses."

Sabina scoffed. "Please, he's a business regulation attorney. The nerds of the big boys. Besides, words hurt Jonathan far worse than physical pain. Trust me, I know, I've spent the last two decades married to him."

"Deep breaths, just like we practiced," Julie told her. "In through your nose, out through your mouth."

Sabina took a right turn down a side street and pulled over to the curb. Shifting the car into park, she did as Julie instructed, closing her eyes for a moment to collect her thoughts. After about a dozen breaths and her anger coming in and out like the tide, she was finally in a calmer state.

"Thank you," Sabina told Julie, grateful that she had someone to help her keep her head on her shoulders. "Jonathan actually owes you, as well. You've kept him from death who knows how many times."

Julie smirked. "I'll bill his office. Now, try to walk in there with a level professionalism that he hasn't seen from you. Remind him that you aren't playing games with your company, that this is for *real*. You don't have to put up with him demeaning your dreams anymore. If he wants out, then let him out, and show him everything that includes. A calm and adult Sabina, ready to tackle the world on her own."

"It's either that or I tackle him, and I would much rather put my life exactly where I want it instead," she replied. "I'll call you later with an update. Thanks again, I appreciate having a best friend with a modicum of understanding of just what I'm going through."

"You got it," Julie replied. "I've been a single mom for a long time and there's been more than one moment of weakness where I wanted to track down Zoey's father and shove him in the garbage disposal. And whoever this boy is—well, I won't get into that right now. Just know that if Zoey even mutters his name in her sleep, we'll need tarps, a shovel, and some bleach."

"Got it ready in the shed," Sabina said and laughed. "Love you."

"Love you, too," Julie said and sighed. "Go be you and remind him how much he'll hate his life with the tart."

"Easy," Sabina scoffed, ending the call.

How much would he hate his life with the tart? It would happen, but not for a while. And trying to compete with a woman that young was just about impossible. Then again, there was no competition. Sabina had gotten a taste of what her life could be and if Jonathan wanted out, he could walk right out the door. Right after signing his name on the dotted line, whether she had to force him to or not.

CHAPTER 2

*I*f Sabina could have held her head any higher as she entered the firm, she would have been staring at the ceiling. She knew pity when she saw it but didn't want it. Walking with purpose through the hallway, she could still remember the first time she visited Jonathan at work. Back when he was actually happy to see her, instead of cringing in apprehension.

Bypassing Gretchen, his secretary, Sabina entered Jonathan's office, closing the door behind her. She dramatically swung around and marched up to his polished cherry desk. She didn't bother with the niceties. She held the loan papers in her hand and slapped them down hard on the desk in front of him. Up to that point, he hadn't even looked up, and even with the breeze from the pound of paperwork she threw down, he only glanced at it for a moment.

Sabina knew Jonathan was ignoring her on purpose, it was one of his games. He knew she hated it, but this time she didn't take the bait. Instead, she went straight to the meat and potatoes of it all. "Where the hell were you?"

He finished his signature on one of the pieces of paper and

placed the pen in his center desk drawer before sitting back, finally looking up at her. He looked distinguished with his silver temples, salt-and-pepper hair and pinstripes. She should have known he was cheating on her when he started dying his mustache. "I was in court," he answered simply.

Sabina pressed her lips firmly together and continued her noisy breaths. "Don't give me that bull—the loan officer said you'd had a change of heart. And if that's true, you lied to me. In exchange for your freedom, you promised me money to help me start my business." She pulled another stack of papers from her bag and waved the copy of the agreement he'd signed in front of his nose.

"I will." He reached over to toggle his mouse, concentrating on his computer's monitor, attempting to avoid eye contact.

Sabina leaned across the desk, staring right into his face. "When?"

Jonathan took in a breath and stood up, tapping a stack of papers on the edge of the desk. "Soon."

Sabina shook her finger at him, giving an irritated frown. "*Now.*"

"Now isn't a good time."

"Well then maybe I should just start unpacking all my stuff," she shrugged, looking down at her fingernails.

Jonathan rolled his eyes, moving around the office to stand at the window to take in the grassy frontage on Linda Avenue beyond—the window he'd coveted for so long. "Don't be so melodramatic. Besides, Courtney's already packing to move in."

Sabina pursed her lips and cocked her head with sass. "And it's *my* name on the deed, not hers."

Jonathan stood back behind his desk, shuffling some papers around, not touching the loan paperwork. "Look, we'll reschedule time for the meeting with the bank," he glanced at his desk calendar. "Next week."

Sabina jammed her finger down on the calendar. "Tomorrow.

I mean it, Jonathan. I will take you to court, I'm fine with that. But I'll go to the media, not to mention social media. That won't endear you to the partners. Remember, I know where the financial bodies are buried."

Jonathan had only made partner the year before, and he still tended to tread softly. His lips pursed, fire igniting behind his hazel eyes.

"All right, tomorrow then. I can clear my schedule after lunch."

Sabina straightened. Victory. But Jonathan wasn't entirely off the hook. She made sure to keep the same intensity, wanting him to know how important their daughter was in all of this.

"Have you told Marisa yet?"

This time he did wince. "I told you, I'd prefer to do it in person."

Sabina let out a growling sigh of frustration. "And I told you it's unfair to spring this news on her when I'm about to move out of the house."

"You could tell her. That kind of news ought to come from her mother," he replied, not even trying to look at her.

Sabina hoped her cold glare froze him right down to his boxers. "Really? The news that *you* asked for a divorce? That *you* asked me to move out so you could move your little chippy in, who happens to be only eight years older than her? That's she's going to be a big sister?" Sabina shook her head and straightened her skirt. "No way in hell."

He winced again. Good.

Jonathan sighed. "I'll tell her. Perhaps this weekend."

Sabina raced around the side of his desk. "No, Jonathan, tonight." She grabbed his arm as he stood and turned him so he faced her. "I'm giving you everything you asked for. The divorce, the house. You can at least hold up your end of the bargain. You need to tell her before she hears it somewhere else, and you need to make sure that she knows she'll still be welcome in the only home she's ever known. This shouldn't affect her any more than is necessary. We already talked about all of this."

His head sank. Marisa had always been daddy's little girl. It served him right that he had to shatter her illusions of him as being supremely perfect.

"I'll see you at the bank tomorrow, Sabina."

Sabina pulled down her suit jacket. "Call her."

Jonathan reclaimed his seat and picked up the phone. "Gretchen, can you get me the Dawson file?"

As she walked to the office door, Sabina remembered the financials. She turned back around, too exhausted to keep up the snarly attitude. "We need to figure out the bank situation soon, as well."

"I already took care of it," he replied, his pen back in his hand, trying to ignore her once again. "You aren't on the accounts anymore."

Sabina stopped in her tracks, her eyes narrowing as she took a step toward him. "You did what?"

"It's easier that way," he replied exhaustively. "But I'm sure you'll make a big deal about that, too."

"You're darn right I will," she said, anger slamming back into her. "You had absolutely no right to do that. They are *joint* accounts and since New York is a community property state, are rightfully half mine." Arms akimbo, she shook her head. "Why am I even having to tell you this? I know your mind has been swimming with dreams of grandeur with your cheap little mistress, but you *are* an attorney. You of all people should understand that. Why are you making decisions like you're completely in the dark?" She threw up her hands and shook her head. "You know what? Never mind. I am not going to fight with you over this. I'll just get my attorney to handle the financial parts. I printed out the statements yesterday, so I know exactly how much was in every one of those accounts."

"You act like I'm trying to starve you," he snarled under his breath.

"Aren't you, Jonathan?" she asked. "End a marriage, take the house, refuse to abide by the contract you signed, take my name off of the accounts, neglect your daughter. Shall I continue?"

He shook his head. "I'll see you later, Sabina."

"You bet you will, because I'm not leaving our home until I get what you promised me. You and your hot toddy can just stay in her cracker-box apartment until that baby she's carrying is ready for retirement."

"Is that a threat?"

"You better believe it."

Jonathan's mouth tightened—and so did his voice. "Fine. I'll see you tomorrow at the bank."

Sabina nodded curtly and left the office with her head held high. She walked past the open doors of some of the other attorneys, knowing every eye was on her. She knew full well that all of them knew what Jonathan was up to long before she did.

What did they think of her now? That she was the poor dumped sap who'd let the office trollop steal her husband? Courtney could have him, but Sabina wanted what he'd promised her to secure his freedom. A bribe perhaps, but a deal was a deal. There would be no negotiation and he was going to start understanding that she wasn't working off of his timeline anymore. She would have what was promised and he could either fall in line, or she was going to run him right over, and his little piece of arm candy, too.

When she got to her car, she sat there in the parking lot, dialing her lawyer. Tonya was a friend of hers and was her family law attorney to boot. Since they'd known each other since they were kids, she was more than happy to help through calls and emails without charging Sabina an arm and a leg.

"Tonya Harbor's office, how can I help you?" the secretary asked on the other end of the line.

For some reason her voice made Sabina cringe and she wondered if she had developed a hatred for young tarts.

"Yes, this is Sabina Mill—um, Sabina Reigns. May I speak to Tonya?"

"I'll see if she's available," the girl replied.

A moment later, "This is Tonya."

Sabina waited, assuming that the very pretty but completely dimwitted secretary didn't know how to work the hold button. She could hear the girl rattling around her desk until finally the other phone was hung up.

"Hey, it's Sabina."

"Oh boy, what's the idiot done now?" Tonya asked, having known Jonathan as long as Sabina had. "Let me guess, he didn't sign the loan."

"Why did everyone see that coming except me?" She shook her head. "No, he didn't, but I pushed him a bit and he rescheduled for tomorrow so I'm not sounding the alarm on that part just yet. He did, however, find the time to take me off of all of our bank accounts."

"Uh, how did he even do that?" Tonya asked. "Banks don't usually agree to that unless you're there to sign."

"Yeah, well, apparently not our bank," Sabina said and groaned, staring at the bags under her eyes in the visor mirror.

Tonya sighed. "All right, well, give it a couple of days and if he doesn't give you something, I'll send him a letter. He doesn't want to go to court. He knows that."

"I know," Sabina replied, slamming the visor up and starting the car. "I just wanted to keep you up to date. I'll call you tomorrow if he doesn't sign the deal."

"I'll be here," Tonya replied.

Stabbing the call-end icon, Sabina tossed her phone into her purse, she pulled out of the parking lot and onto the road, heading back to the house. It was almost painful to go back there. It wasn't because of the memories or the nostalgia of her perfectly curated designs within. It was the reminder that she had to find a place, afford that place, and get her stuff out so her younger replacement could seamlessly step right in and take over as though time inside the home had been rewound by eighteen years. Though, Sabina really didn't see Courtney as the kind of girl—and she deliberately used the word—to stick it out through the monumental amount of crap a man like Jonathan put a wife through.

Sabina drove the familiar route back to the house, almost on autopilot. She pulled up to the garage and got out, standing there staring at the house for just one emotional moment. When she was done, she sliced her hands through the air and nodded astutely. "That's it, that's all I get. It's just a house, I'll own another one day."

She felt lucky in a way. The stench of Jonathan's deceit was so thick in that house it was hard to be forlorn about leaving. Except for the fact she still didn't have another place to go. She wasn't worried though, Sabina knew it wouldn't take long to find a temporary spot to stay, especially since Marisa would continue living at the house. All she needed was a kitchen, a bathroom, and somewhere to rest her head. The décor would be easy, that was her specialty.

Once inside, Sabina roamed through the living room, feeling almost uncomfortable in her own home. It felt like rejection. As though she was being balled up and tossed out. She stood at the fireplace staring at a picture of her family, the three of them when Marisa was just a little girl. She picked up the frame and held her thumb over Jonathan's face, smiling at how Marisa used to cling to her. It was a photo of a trip they'd taken to Niagara Falls. Simpler times, good times. At least they had that... once upon a time.

The question that lingered in the back of Sabina's mind was if she would ever have that again. Or had it ever really existed at all?

CHAPTER 3

"*I*'ve met someone else."

Those four simple words had unceremoniously ended Sabina's twenty-year marriage. Not that they came as a surprise. Jonathan had been working late nights, early mornings, and weekends for quite some time now. And he had 'met someone else' two or three times before during the years they'd been together. This time was different, though. There was a finality to it that was very quickly summed up in just two words with no further explanation required.

"She's pregnant."

Sabina's stomach lurched and she nearly dropped her coffee cup as she stared at Jonathan across the breakfast table. Her eyelids blinked at a rapid pace and she pouted, pulled back, and then pouted again, feeling as though her body was moving without her consent. It was a twitch, a discombobulated reaction to two sentences she didn't know what to make of.

Her eyes shifted up toward the ceiling, not wanting to see Jonathan watch her as though she were going to have a stroke right there at the table. After her nerves had finished dancing the samba, she stared back at him, lips tight and very little expression behind her eyes. "Who?"

He took a deep breath and glanced down at his plate. She wished he would be more assertive. If you were going to cheat, knock a girl up, and leave your wife for her, you had better damn well be sure that's what you want.

"My associate, Courtney Sullivan."

Pretty, blonde, and twenty-something, Courtney worked as a paralegal in Jonathan's law office. Sabina had met her once or twice. Even entertained the bitch in her home. The little hussy.

"I want to be with her—and the baby." The latter part of that statement almost sounded like an afterthought. Their own daughter was in her first semester of college. Marisa had always been closer to her father, so it was with a sense of relief that Sabina had carefully packed for her daughter and taken her to the airport just the day before Jonathan's announcement. No doubt he'd been waiting for her to leave to drop his bomb at breakfast.

Before Sabina had time to digest the first salvo, he launched another. "I want to keep the house."

Well, he was just full of little announcements. Probably more requests than he had made in their whole twenty years of marriage. Too bad they were for some other woman. But the house? Her showcase of a house? The same house he did nothing but complain about because Sabina used it as her canvas, constantly updating the décor? It was her muse, her blank slate with each and every change of season. She had done more practice in that house for her interior design work then she had actually done work for clients.

She only had one question.

"Why do you want the house?"

Jonathan shrugged, sipping his coffee. "It's conveniently located near the office, and I don't want to live anywhere else. Besides, it's perfect."

A compliment. She hadn't expected that.

"I promise," he continued. "I'll give you your share of the full market value. Call in whoever you like for the appraisal."

But she had a more important question on her mind. It was funny to her that after twenty years her thought process on what he was saying was very short, pretty emotionless—though that could be shock—and rather uncaring. They were sitting there, sipping coffee, conversing as though they were discussing what restaurant to go to for dinner. Or at least he was, Sabina was holding everything inside like she usually did. She knew he could smell weaknesses like a wild animal.

"What about Marisa?" Sabina asked. "Who's going to tell her?"

He glanced nervously at her for a moment and then back down at his cup. "Well, naturally, I assumed you would."

She shook her head. "I'm not the one asking for the divorce. And, you can't expect me to tell her about her new little brother or sister, either."

Jonathan frowned. "I suppose you're right. I'll get to it in the next couple of days."

The blinking started again, this time slower and more purposeful. "Do I need to remind you that this is Marisa's home, too?"

He shrugged. "Now that she's in college, I'm sure she'll—"

Sabina interrupted him quickly, not even allowing him to go there. "Be home for holidays and summers. You don't expect her to just up and find another place to live, do you?"

"Of course not. She'll always be welcome here." He spoke about his own daughter as though she were some guest or a family friend.

There was a silence between them for several moments. Sabina leaned back in the chair, her eyes narrowed, her arms crossed in defense. "And how does Courtney feel about sharing her home with your college-age daughter."

"We've discussed it."

They'd discussed it? He'd apparently discussed a lot more

with Courtney than he had with Sabina. Maybe that was why he was talking to her as though he hadn't just completely turned their world upside down.

When Sabina didn't have any more questions, Jonathan finished his coffee and put the mug in the sink. Suddenly everything about him made Sabina want to vomit. The handsome man she had once thought about as her husband had been replaced by someone else—a complete stranger.

He grabbed his briefcase and for a moment she thought he was going to pause for his usual goodbye kiss. Instead, he glanced at the refrigerator and the papers stuck to it with Marisa's cheerful and quirky Mary Englebreit magnets.

"Do we have to have all this crap up here?"

Sabina didn't even care to look back at the fridge, wondering why he even felt the need to comment on it. She stood and followed him to the door, standing several feet back as he walked out. She stayed put, watching him walk down the sidewalk, key fob in hand. He entered the garage and the big double door rose. He pulled his car out and revved it up. His getaway ride.

Sabina closed the door, not particularly angry and not even all that numb. As she cleared the table and stood over the sink scraping an egg-stained dish, Sabina thought about her feelings. Or lack thereof. By the time the dish was in the dishwasher she had decided that 'oddly detached' would be a more accurate assessment of her emotional state. Like clockwork, she reached down and picked up Jonathan's dirty dish and turned the water on. The soiled plate in her hands was yet another reminder of how Jonathan and she had never really meshed. He liked his eggs poached—runny; she liked hers hard.

She was still pondering his request to keep the house and move Courtney into it. What a strange feeling it was to be told by your husband that your replacement had arrived and it was time for you to move on. He said it as though it was a normal part of life. Like he had gone to the wife store and ordered the next round, this one younger, firmer, and livelier than his 'older version' had been.

Part of her wanted to spite him—and make him fight tooth and nail for the platform of her talents. The house she had put her soul into more than once, sometimes more than once a day even. The place she always felt comfortable, and the place where she got her best ideas. Sabina thought she loved it as much as she loved Jonathan. Now, she wasn't so sure. It was a toss-up really, especially with the sudden haze of surprise and dismay that lingered in the air like fog.

As she loaded the dishwasher on that gray morning, Sabina glanced at the papers littering the front of the fridge. Most of them were Marisa's school lists. She took them down, carefully folding them, not that she needed them anymore. A ray of sunlight broke through the gloom and shone upon a note she'd almost forgotten she'd tacked up there. An invitation to bid on the Parkview Mansion renovation. Sabina hadn't seriously considered it—until that very moment.

A bit of Irish pique erupted in her. If Jonathan was determined to start a new life, why shouldn't she? Maybe this was the golden opportunity she'd been waiting for. Could she take the lemons he handed her and make lemonade?

Jonathan had always resisted the idea of Sabina having her own business. Staying home with their daughter was her job; he'd insisted on that with fervor. Playing Mommy was fine for the first five years, but when Marisa started kindergarten Sabina had gone back to college and earned her post-graduate degree in interior design. Over the years she'd worked part-time for several firms in the area but hadn't yet developed a clientele of her own. She didn't think the opportunity for her own clients would surface for quite a long time.

One day though, she'd promised herself, she would have a shop of her own. Natural light, a sumptuous showroom with living and dining room sets, crystal chandeliers, fabric samples filling cubbies on the back wall, and a fabulous drawing board. It would be everything she had pictured in her mind and more. The place that had grown and changed, matured over time and eventually became perfected in her brain over the last twenty-some years. That was one hell of a long time to hold onto a dream and still have some sort of hope for fulfillment.

She pushed the dishwasher's on button and found her mood lightening as the possibilities for her future burst before her mind's eye in complete and exquisite detail. And the crown jewel would be the Parkview Manor renovation. It would be her first substantial client, her golden egg. It would be the showcase to preserve her place among the affluent in the vicinity. She would be the woman they went to for a creative and comfortable home, one of a kind, structured and shaped just for them.

She snatched the paperwork off the fridge. Yikes! The deadline was only a week away. Could she pull something like that together in such a short period of time?

Sabina took the stairs two at a time, heading for the shower. There was a lot of brainstorming and creating to do and not very much time. She'd show Jonathan that she could be a success. That she really didn't need him.

Lemonade never sounded so good.

* * *

PARKVIEW MANOR FACED the broad boulevard within spitting distance of Highland Park, home of one of the world's largest lilac collections. In better times, the once-elegant home was considered a fine example of a Greek Revival. Now the rotting shutters, missing downspouts, peeling paint and cracked, stained or missing slate tiles on the roof, said a lot about the exterior. As she stared up at the rotted soffit, she cringed at the thought of what she'd find inside. She was glad she'd taken the time to research and begin planning.

The door was unlocked. Sabina stepped inside the old house and felt a pang of regret at the noticeable neglect. Water stained ceilings, faded wallpaper, and old crown molding missing from near the ceiling reinforced her initial assessment. The thread-bare, ragged carpets were probably older than her parents.

An elderly woman, wearing a bulky knitted sweater, dark wool skirt, and sensible shoes, entered the foyer. "I thought I heard someone come in. May I help you?"

Sabina held out her hand. "Sabina Mi—" she stopped herself. Miller was her married name. If Jonathan was going to give it to Courtney, she figured she'd better go back to her *real* name. "Sabina Reigns. I've been invited to submit a bid on the Parkview renovation."

The woman's wrinkled brow furrowed deeper. "I'm sorry. I don't recall that we solicited an invitation to anyone by that name."

Sabina showed the woman her paperwork and briefly explained.

She nodded. "I see. Only one other person is waiting to take the tour. It will begin in fifteen minutes. Perhaps you'd like to read through our brochure while you wait." She handed Sabina a badly done tri-fold photocopy leaflet and left her standing in the drafty hall.

The only chair in the entryway had a piece of gold cord draped across the arms, blocking the seat. She'd have to stand.

Sabina scanned the brochure. Built in 1840, Parkview Manor had sixteen rooms, twelve of which were furnished in the once-popular Empire style and were open to the public. Tremendous efforts had been made to acquire as many of the home's original furnishings as possible. Other pieces were original to the period with most dating from 1820 to 1850, the height of the Empire Period.

"Sabina Miller?"

She looked up to find a tall, dark-haired young man in a

three-piece, pin-striped suit, looking like he would make a better companion to Courtney than her soon-to-be former husband. He held out a limp hand and she had to force herself to shake it.

"Actually, I'm now Sabina Reigns."

The young man raised an eyebrow but refrained from commenting. "Todd Foreman, personal assistant to Charles Patterson. I believe you two are acquainted."

Oh, yes. Well acquainted. Sabina forced a smile. "And what are you doing here?"

Todd rubbed his finger along the banister of the staircase, inspected it, and frowned. "Slumming. When Charles wins the contract, I'll be in charge of seeing that everything runs smoothly."

His audacity was shocking, though she wasn't sure why as Charles Patterson was a complete asshole—why shouldn't his associate display the same arrogance? "I understood the decision would be made within a month of the filing deadline."

Todd gave a forced smile and strolled along, waving his hand to his side as he looked up and down the walls. "Oh yes, but it's a foregone conclusion that Charles Patterson Associates will win."

Oh yeah?

Sabina plastered on her most patronizing grin. "Do tell."

* * *

JONATHAN DIDN'T COME HOME that evening, not that Sabina expected him to. He hadn't been home since he broke the news. It was all the better and gave her time to enjoy those last few fleeting moments in her home without wanting to throw up at the mere sight of Jonathan. On the one hand she wished he would just forget about the house and never come back. On the other hand, she needed that severe and painful break to move on. She couldn't sit in the past any longer.

The e-mail Sabina received from Marisa that night made no

mention of the separation and Sabina didn't comment on it in her reply. Jonathan could do his own dirty work.

And she was determined not to sit around pining for him.

Having dreamed about her own business for as long as she could remember, Sabina already had a business plan, and it had been reworked, perfected, and reworded a hundred times over the last three years. Every couple of months Sabina would take it out and polish it. On nights Jonathan worked late, she'd draw and redraw her ideas for a combination shop and studio. So, when it came to getting a business loan, she wasn't like everyone else. The loan was the last step, and she had been ready as soon as the idea came to mind.

Now all she had to do was hope Jonathan showed up the next day. Otherwise, homicide might be her new focus. The loan was important, very important. It had been an initial thought when she first threw it out there but now, it was vital to her future. It was what would give her life meaning again. A salve for the burn she felt from Jonathan's choices and the series of reactions they had caused. She thought about what his face must have looked like when Courtney gave him the news. A new baby, wow. What a responsibility.

She shook her head, reminding herself that he was the enemy and there was no reason for her to be considering his feelings any longer. It was a hard habit to break, but she knew that she needed to if for no other reason than to maintain her own sanity, and her ability to put on a brave face with Marisa.

Daddy's girl or not, her daughter was a firecracker, a wild girl with new-age ideas of love. She would not be happy to hear of her father's infidelity, and there was no other way to explain the story. A pregnant woman moving into her childhood home would be obvious enough.

The next morning, Sabina's phone rang. She picked it up after studying the name displayed. Julie was more than likely worried because Sabina had not sent her normal flurry of texts the day before. "Well, hello there, No Answer Angela."

With a forced smile, she gathered herself. Julie was going to freak out, Sabina knew it. She could feel it in her bones. "Are we still on for lunch?"

"That's why I was calling, to make sure we were still on," Julie replied, her words faltering a bit. "Are you okay? You sound a little, well, off somehow."

"Actually, I'm not sure," Sabina replied.

"Uh-oh," she said. "I'll meet you there soon."

Sabina was about to unleash a hailstorm of angry sisterhood, but it was good. Julie pushed her, and Sabina was going to need that as she navigated the success or failure of this new life and career ahead of her. Julie was supportive though hard on Sabina, but sometimes, that tough love was exactly what she needed. A slap in the face followed by some really good advice.

Sabina was happy to have such a friend.

CHAPTER 4

*D*uring the next few days, Sabina spent most of her time at the house going through her possessions, assembling piles of items destined for charity, tossing what she no longer needed and packing what she did, while staying as far away from Memory Lane as she possibly could. She had finally taken the time to sit down with multiple furniture catalogs to decide exactly what she wanted for her new apartment. It was just the pick me up she needed.

Sabina found a small sublet not far from the upscale strip mall where she hoped to open her showroom. It wasn't the pits, but not much better. She had her sights on the big picture and figured she could accept a bit of hardship for some delayed gratification.

The next order of business was for Sabina to pack up her home studio—what Jonathan insisted on calling her 'little sewing room.' He'd always considered her work more of a hobby, maybe even a joke, than a real job.

Along with the sewing machine and drawing board, she packed her files, her books, swatches, and what seemed like too little of her life. It was dividing up the photographs that made the whole idea of the separation real to her. Not just a separation. Jonathan would be replacing her with a young blonde trophy wife, and she was making it easy for him.

Yet New York's laws required a one-year separation phase before a divorce could be granted. Courtney wouldn't be sporting a new last name until after she gave birth to the little Miller bastard.

Still, Sabina found herself counting the days until she could get out of her lifeless marriage and even more lifeless lifestyle. Still, the memories those photos evoked—of newborn Marisa, and the parties and holidays Jonathan and she had shared—squeezed her heart until she felt breathless and scared.

Sabina selected the photos she wanted for herself, figuring she could always scan them and crop Jonathan out. Then she packed up the rest, stowing the box on the top shelf in Marisa's bedroom closet. They were hers now.

Since she'd left the state, Marisa had become a much better communicator, texting several times a day and occasionally sending entire emails. Sabina was pleased that the two-hundred-plus-mile distance between them actually seemed to heal the rift between them that formed during adolescence. It was obvious that Jonathan hadn't told their daughter about their impending separation. Sabina had no intention of breaking the news to the girl, but she wasn't going to keep what she was doing a secret, either.

MISSY,

I've had an amazing day. I finally picked out all new bedroom furniture and decided on a gorgeous couch and chair, chintz cottagey stuff that is wonderfully homey and cozy. I hope you'll love it when you see it. I'm off to buy new linens tomorrow. I want to do the bedroom in English country cottage as well. The idea of settling in and cocooning really appeals to me right now.

But the bigger news is that I've decided to open my own design studio. I've got my heart set on opening a shop in the big plaza in Pittsford.

More news as it happens.

Love you,

Mom

WRITING THAT EMAIL FELT GOOD. She wished Marisa knew the whole truth so she could open up completely, but this would have to do for now. At least Sabina could finally show her daughter her superpowers. She could show Marisa that being a woman was more than just washing dishes and 'playing at' decorating the house over and over again. Of course, she felt like she had shown her daughter more than that as she was growing up, but once Sabina discovered that new freedom, that independence of a grown woman not tied to anything but her almost-adult daughter, she began to question some of what she had taught the girl.

One of the things Sabina had always admired about Julie and Zoey was that Julie had taken the reins when her husband left her. She had come out of the shadows, not that she had ever hidden in them very well, but she emerged as this strong, feisty, and killer role model for her daughter. Sabina knew Julie didn't really see it that way since Zoey had gotten pregnant so young, but to Sabina, that had nothing to do with what Julie had done with her life. It was a direct reflection of the turmoil a divorce could have on a young girl. Zoey still had a full life ahead of her, and one that she would, without knowing it, tackle with a certain fervor and passion, just as Julie had done. Or at least that was what everyone hoped for.

Now, Sabina had the same hope for Marisa. While she was three years older than Zoey, she still had her whole life ahead of her. Sabina wanted to impart her life lessons, her experiences to her daughter, and raise her to expect and embrace the unexpected, no matter how painful and scary it may seem early on. A little dose of reality in Marisa's sugar-coated childhood wouldn't be so bad, even if it felt catastrophic at first.

Sabina let out a deep sigh and closed her laptop, staring around the room. It felt hollow, losing its former import by the minute. For the first time since Jonathan had asked for a divorce, Sabina felt more than ready to leave that house—and that life—in the dust. Maybe Courtney could pick up her pieces and find some sort of happiness in it.

But hopefully not.

The golden September days melted into one another. Two weeks after Jonathan's announcement, Sabina moved out of their lovely colonial-style home and the adventure really began.

* * *

"LET'S SEE, that's the bedroom suite, the couch, end tables, two chairs and an ottoman. And how will you be paying for this?" the salesman asked, as he completed his order form.

Sabina handed him her new credit card, thankful that Jonathan had actually shown up weeks before to sign the loan paperwork, otherwise all the furniture would have been inflatable or chipboard. The loan signing had been a rather painless experience to her surprise, but apparently painful for him. He was only there about five minutes, swishing his illegible signature across the lines of the contract before giving her a pained look and stalking out. Sabina found the scenario more than satisfying.

She smiled at the salesman. "Will delivery on the fly be a problem?"

"Not at all. Excuse me, while I run this through. It'll only take a moment."

Sabina sat back in the comfortable cushioned chair. As a regular Stickley customer, she often spent tens of thousands on furniture for her clients. It felt good to buy something just for herself.

Her new furniture was much too good for the basement sublet just off bustling Monroe Avenue. A bedroom, a galley kitchen/living room combination and a bathroom smaller than her former walk-in closet. The price was right she told herself, and it was just a place to sleep. With any luck, she'd be pouring her life into starting the business anyway. That would be the balm for her soul. The apartment was just a place to temporarily rest her head.

"If you could fill out this delivery form, we'll be all set. We'll call to touch base the day before," the salesman explained, handing Sabina a clipboard and pen.

"Thank you," she replied, suddenly realizing the embarrassment she'd feel to see that beautiful furniture delivered to what was essentially a dump. Granted, the guys with the dollies would just be delivery boys, most likely college kids trying to make a few bucks to buy beer and pizza, but they'd be cramming expensive furniture into her ridiculously small and cheesy apartment.

Sabina decided there and then that she was going to have to learn not to care. She wanted to be comfortable, and tight budgets were the reality of her future. She was going to need that, no matter what contracts she got at first. She handed back the clipboard and stuck her clutch under her arm, smiling as she left the showroom.

"Off to the house—apartment, I mean," she said to herself. "Come on Sabina, just go home before you start having a full-blown conversation with yourself in public again."

She drove across the county to the apartment, letting herself in and tossing her keys in the small ornate porcelain bowl she had purchased before the crushing news had been rolled out like a nasty old carpet. It was one of the first things she snatched up before she left the house she'd shared with Jonathan. She hadn't even put it out for display in the house and was not going to let Jonathan and his slutty prego girlfriend get anywhere near it.

Walking into her barren apartment, Sabina stared at the boxes of piecemeal belongings she'd packed in the back of her SUV and taken from the house. It was only a fraction of the twenty years of décor, personal items, and clothing she had put together over the years, but they were incredibly important to her. She had to keep reminding herself that it was just stuff. In her new life, she'd acquire plenty more, and those random dozen or so boxes would slowly filter themselves out or be packed up and stored away for Marisa when she got a place of her own after she graduated from college. Until then, Sabina would make do with what she had.

The smart thing would have been to start unpacking as best she could, but Sabina was exhausted, more mentally than physically. The one living room chair she managed to swipe from the old homestead looked inviting, but her Ilminster wing back would just have to wait. The temporary inflatable mattress in her bedroom was calling her, at least after a hot and reaffirming shower.

Kicking off her shoes, Sabina began to pull off her earrings, necklace, and bracelet. As she looked at the clasp, the shimmer of her diamond engagement ring caught her attention. She put her bracelet in the jewelry box currently sitting on the box of linens she had brought, then held up her hand, remembering the first time she struck that pose after laying her eyes on the shimmering two carats. The mood had been a bit brighter and far more celebratory during the initial glance, but all the emotion still stuck with Sabina, somewhere deep in her trove of two decades of memories. All of that was now history, and everything had to change in order to put it in the past. Sabina knew that, even if difficult was a word she was getting tired of using.

With a sigh she gripped her finger and slid the ring and its companion gold band off, tossing them in her palm for just a moment. It felt like the real end. Like everything else had merely been in preparation for that moment. She had thought the reality would come with the swish of a pen against the stack of divorce papers, but she had only ever removed her engagement and wedding rings one time before, during a minor surgery to remove her appendix. This time it was voluntary and signified the end of her old life and the beginning of her new one.

Sabina looked around her bedroom, absorbing the stark chill of the empty walls and bare floors. Moving aside years of birthday and anniversary gifts received in the form of jewelry, she stowed her wedding band at the bottom of the box. She wasn't sure what she wanted to do with her engagement ring. Though large, the stone was flawed—all Jonathan could afford at the time. Maybe she would have it reset in a necklace for Marisa for her birthday or Christmas.

It was a nice idea, but Sabina wasn't sure if Marisa would be ready for something like that since she didn't even know about the divorce. The finality of such a gift might be too much for her. But one day, hopefully. Who knew? Maybe Marisa might even want it for her own engagement ring. By that point in life, the sentimental value would rest solely with her, remnants of a relationship she only saw in the positive eyes of a child. For everyone else, the memories and emotions had faded. Then again, Marisa might very well hate Sabina, and tell her exactly where she could stick her cursed diamond.

Either way, Sabina was going to hold onto it for now, leaving it in the dark recesses of her jewelry box, waiting for the day to see it sparkle again. Hopefully, the next time she saw it it wouldn't have such dramatic and despondent overtones. It was a diamond after all, and flawed or not, still a woman's best friend.

Sabina allowed herself a bemused smile, thinking about that sentiment. While it was meant as a marketing ploy for guys, it kind of rang true. When the lust and happiness drained from a marriage, women were still able to enjoy the sparkle of their favorite stone for decades to come.

"Maybe the slogan should say, 'Diamonds, guaranteed to outlast even your marriage,'" Sabina whispered to herself with a shake of her head as she closed the jewelry box.

She changed into linen shorts and a tank top, then carefully laid down on her inflatable mattress. She had at least covered it with six-hundred thread-count sheets and tried to think of it as sleeping on her parents' waterbed from when she was a child, only not wavy. With this one, she had to roll off of it and pull herself up off the floor, a stark reminder that her body wasn't quite as spry as the last time she was single.

"It's only for another couple of days," she repeated to herself. It was a repetition that had become like a new mantra for her. It was a few more days until her new life could finally begin.

CHAPTER 5

"Oh, Sabina, you can't be serious," Julie wailed.

Sabina held open the door to her new apartment with her foot, juggling her purse, keys, and a box of new dishes, waiting for her friend to pass through.

"Home sweet home," Sabina assured her, having gotten used to the place now that a few days had passed.

Devoid of furniture and decoration, the empty space still smelled of fresh paint, while triangular vacuum cleaner tracks decorated the beige carpet. For a moment, Sabina was afraid that Julie might cry. For days, Sabina had forced herself to look at the place as a blank canvas, but she could understand the shock of it for someone who had never seen it before, especially compared to the masterpiece she had created in her former home. Nonetheless, Sabina wouldn't let Julie's reaction dampen her enthusiasm, not yet, not until after she had done everything she could to warm up the space. After all, what kind of decorator would she be if she couldn't make that hovel inviting and livable? The tiny, ugly apartment would be a true testament to her decorating skill.

Julie had yet to come through the door, stuck in shock just outside, as though entering would spiral her into another dimension. "You gave up your beautiful home for this?" she cried, anguished.

"Of course not. I gave it up for my shop. But I have to live somewhere. And it's only a sublet. I'll be out of here in six months. Now, hurry up. My arms are about to fall off."

Tilting her head to the side and lifting her eyebrows in worry, Julie barreled over the threshold, her own arms laden with a bulky cardboard carton filled with clothes—one of the last of the boxes from Sabina's former home. They dumped the boxes on the breakfast bar and gazed around the room. She shook her head doubtfully.

"Jonathan's an idiot. It's not like you let yourself go." Julie brushed a piece of lint from Sabina's blue linen jacket. "I wish I could still get into size eight jeans."

Ten actually, but Sabina left Julie to her illusions.

Sabina shrugged, wiping a layer of dust off the counter and brushing her hands together. "Come on, it's an adventure."

Julie raised an eyebrow. "No, a week in a hostel in Jamaica during spring break was an adventure. This is a dorm room."

With a sigh and roll of her eyes, Sabina started to take her clothes out of the box. "It's not like it's forever. Besides, you know me, I can make any space work. It'll be so comfortable by the time I move out that you'll want to rent it just to get away from it all."

Staring up at the boob light above their heads, laden with insect carcasses, Julie wrinkled her nose. "Somehow, I doubt that, but hey, if you're happy then I support you. I guess you don't need that much space right now anyway with Marisa still having her spot back at the old house."

"Exactly," Sabina said and nodded. "Think about my first place before I married Jonathan. It may have been bigger, but I shared it with a cockroach so big I named him Buddy."

Julie laughed. "Oh yeah. I wonder whatever happened to Buddy."

"He probably took over the lease," Sabina said and laughed.

Julie shivered at the thought, then gave the room another disparaging glance. "It definitely will be fun to see what you can do with this place."

"How long can you stay?" Sabina asked, folding a pair of pants and setting them on the counter in a neat stack.

Julie glanced down at her watch. "Not long. I have a big job tonight, but I'll be free all day tomorrow."

Sabina clapped her hands excitedly as she grabbed her laptop from the counter. "Good, you can help me start looking at properties. I've got my heart set on a storefront in Pittsford. They have several openings, but I should look at everything that's available in the vicinity just the same."

A knock on the doorjamb distracted them. Sabina crossed the living room in eight steps and glanced through the steel door's peephole before throwing it open. A burly man clutched a clipboard. "Mrs. Sabina Miller? You expecting some furniture?"

Julie scowled. "Miller? You're not keeping *his* name I hope."

"Someone else will be using it soon," Sabina agreed. She'd been waiting to tell someone and was glad Julie was the first. "Actually, as of today, I'm using my *real* name."

Sabina offered the delivery guy her hand. "My name is Sabina Reigns, and yes I am expecting new furniture."

Dressed in gray overalls, his belly far exceeding the limit of the straining seams around the zipper, the delivery guy, just blinked at them. Sabina grinned at him, waiting for some sort of affirmation but when he just continued to blink, Sabina dropped the smile and grabbed the clipboard, dashing off a signature that included both names.

She handed him the clipboard. "Here you go. Bedroom furniture goes in the back room, and the rest in here."

"Be careful, the place is huge, like that purse Mary Poppins had, you could get lost for days," Julie called out with sarcasm.

"Don't mind her. My friend has a unique sense of humor."

"Yeah," he grumbled, unamused. "Be right back."

Sabina turned to Julie with a grin. Julie lifted her eyebrows and shook her head, laughing. She leaned against the door frame and a piece of the wood shifted, falling to the ground. Quickly, she picked it up and handed it to Sabina as she walked out of the apartment. "I'll see you tomorrow. Call me if the ceiling collapses."

Sabina looked down at the piece of wood and shrugged, looking around with a grin. It wasn't going to be too bad, right? It would be home before she knew it.

She hoped.

* * *

THREE DAYS LATER, after picking up the last of her things from her former home, Sabina kicked the door closed behind her and sat the box on the floor. Stretching, she rubbed her lower back and looked around.

She'd organized everything, set out a few knick-knacks, added a throw and some cushions, and the kitchen now was stuffed with everything she could fit into it, but still, it definitely didn't wow her. In fact, she had three really good adjectives to describe it. Cold, inhospitable—*NOT MINE*.

Sabina hadn't thought to buy a television. Back home, she rarely turned it on. She didn't have a stereo, only an old boom box from her home office and a pile of CDs—mostly new-age discs she used as white noise while she worked. Jonathan preferred to sit in silence during the evenings. Though she'd grown used to it, Sabina mourned the absence of joyful noise during the decades. And too much quiet gave Sabina far too much time to sit and ruminate about things she couldn't change. She attempted to keep herself busy, but seeing how small the space was, she could only rearrange the furniture so many times before there were no more options. She had gone through all of her boxes, and even that didn't take her long. Buying a television —if only to hear other voices—was starting to move up on her list of priorities. At the same time though, she knew when she got everything together with her shop, she would have more than enough to do to keep herself occupied.

Her pictures, prints, and paintings were still stacked against the wall. Her lease said no nails, and she still hadn't gotten around to buying Command Strips. The fridge was nearly empty —except for a bottle of Coke, the remains of an old pizza, and milk to add to her morning cup of tea. The French-milled lilac-scented soap sat on the side of the bathroom vanity, gumming up the surface because she didn't have a soap dish.

Sabina had lived in her home for so long she had neglected to think about the small things that made life just a little more enjoyable, like a toothbrush holder and a soap dish. Her shower was packed full, every ledge holding something, with no orga-nizer to hang over the shower head. She had always liked to take baths, but her apartment just had a stand-up shower so she attempted to relax in other ways. She wasn't allowed to burn candles, so she simmered fragrant oils in a mini crock pot on the kitchen counter. What she hadn't thought about though, was how strong the smell was and how small of a space she was working with. You could smell the fragrance ten feet outside the front door.

"It's just temporary, just temporary," she repeated to herself over and over as she stood in the doorway of her bedroom looking out at the living room and kitchen.

While the words had calmed her before, they didn't seem to work anymore. She flexed her fists open and closed, not angrily, but in an attempt to capture that anxiety she was feeling and put it to better use. But as the minutes and hours passed by, the anxiety started to roll and snowball, tainting her mild thoughts with rage. Everything was focused on Jonathan and his little tart, Courtney. While Sabina stood in her tiny apartment, knowing it would nearly fit in the living room of her old house, Courtney wallowed in the lap of luxury, taking advantage of all the hard work Sabina had put into making her previous house a home. She felt put out and cheated, aware that the bitter ex-wife persona was scratching at the surface, begging to be set free.

Sabina had prided herself on the fact that she had handled the separation with grace and dignity. Even in the silence and privacy of her new digs, with no roving eyes to watch her, she felt she'd done well. Every time sadness or regret tried to overwhelm her, she reminded herself that none of it was her fault. That she had done the best she could at being a mother and a wife. But on that day, there was nothing she could do to convince herself that the pain of having her life completely turned upside down in the blink of an eye could ever feel right.

Sometimes, even the strongest people find themselves in situations they can't control. Sabina had repressed her emotions and let her natural self-defense mechanisms push painful things away and continue on. From the moment that Jonathan said the words, "I found someone else," Sabina's emotions had taken a backseat and she found her life running on autopilot. It wasn't until she found herself alone, surrounded by silence, and suffocated by both the seedy apartment and the enormous weight of separation and the inevitable divorce pushing down on her, that she realized just how inconsequential her new furniture was in comparison to the colossal steps she was being forced to take in order to start this new life she had never really asked for.

Sabina had taken a bad situation and found the best in it. Instead of being fearful of the unknown, she looked at a fresh start as exciting and riveting. She'd jumped into it headfirst, without looking back. But as time passed, she was like any other person, inclined to find herself overwhelmed by being so small in such a big world. Her situation was not unique, and there wasn't a magic pot of gold at the end of the divorce rainbow. The reality was, she was starting a business from scratch, living out of a tiny apartment that despite her goal to leave in six months, she might be stuck in for a long time, and she had to face it all alone. After twenty years with someone by her side, the idea of walking into the unknown all alone was frightening.

It had been a long time since anything so devastating had happened to her. Looking back and taking away those last few unsatisfying years with Jonathan where he was constantly absent, constantly in the ear of another woman, Sabina had lived a rather privileged life. She never had to worry about paying bills; Jonathan had always provided. She never had to worry about not working on perfecting her craft—the money was there to afford it. They didn't have drama with difficult friends, and except for the usual mother-daughter squabbles, Marisa had been pretty much perfect her entire life. Okay, she experienced the normal teenage angst, but it was nothing like the horror stories Sabina had heard from other mothers in her sphere. Anything that came about with any sort of negative consequence or emotional drain was handled in stride because the rest of Sabina's world was so tranquil. Until that security was no longer there, Sabina had never given it a thought, she coasted through life like she always had.

As she cast her gaze upon the lackluster walls, a tidal wave of emotion and the sheer gravity of the changes in her life bombarded her, leaving her breathless and bereft. She put a hand on her chest, trying to breathe as deeply as she could, but in the end, Sabina couldn't deflect the rolling boulder of negativity that finally caught up with her.

She stood in the middle of her living room and cried.

CHAPTER 6

"So, this is the showroom that's first on your list?" Julie asked as they walked into the large open space while the Realtor moved to the back of the building to flip on the lights.

Sabina walked slowly through the front door, trying to keep her excitement at bay. She knew that she needed to make a smart choice, not just a choice based on what she had pictured in her mind. If she wanted to be able to fill the place with everything she'd always dreamed of for her shop, she needed to make a decision based on finances as well as location and square footage. The showroom they toured was a bit above the budget she planned, but between the location and the average income of the residents in the area, Sabina calculated that—fingers crossed— she would be able to maintain the space with just two clients a month.

Given the fact that she had never had her own brick-and-mortar store, the idea of luring two new clients a month was a bit daunting. However, after spending more than twenty years preparing for just that, and doing freelance on the side, she had worked with enough clients that she was pretty sure she could not only use existing contacts but pull referrals from those people as well. And then there was the retail aspect. It was a risk no matter which way she looked at it. If she went with space that cost less in an area with a lower median income, she risked not having any clients at all which would make the lower rental fee a moot point because she wouldn't be able to pay it either way, at least not after the loan money ran out.

Sabina took in a long deep breath and looked up at the high ceilings above her. She scanned the area, seeing that it was definitely going to need a complete overhaul, but at least it had a working bathroom, a large storage room at the back, and was a clean slate.

"It's exactly how I imagined it," she said, as she walked past Julie, looking down at the tired old tile floors beneath their feet. "All of this will have to come up, shelving would have to come in, and different structures would have to be built throughout, but that's pretty much true at every place we've looked at."

Julie nodded. "I agree. This is a great location. You can catch the interest of those in the area with higher incomes as well as pulling in clients from other areas willing to drive to the nicer zip code when looking for a designer. The last place was definitely bigger and cheaper though."

Sabina bit the inside of her cheek. "Yes. But I'd prefer to be on this side of the county."

Julie laughed. "Basically, you're saying that the rich people don't want to drive to the poor area and burden themselves with the hassle."

Sabina snapped her fingers and pointed at her friend. "It's a sad realization, but it's true. I mean, it's not like everyone doesn't do that. Whether you're of low or median income, you'll always choose to stay where you're most comfortable. I would say that wealthier people are the worst when it comes to that."

Beverly, the real estate agent walked up, crossing her perfectly manicured fingers in front of her deep purple skirt suit as she glanced around. "I would have to agree with you. Selling homes in this area, I get the question all the time of whether certain stores or parks are located within the same area, and it's not because they don't want to drive, it's because they don't want to go into areas where they don't feel comfortable. This location is well known, the stores well-frequented, and it's easy to get in and out of. This just came on the market a couple of days ago, and probably won't be available for long. The plaza is eager to fill the space and the price is more than reasonable."

After checking out the entire building and going over the terms of the lease, Sabina took a moment and walked outside, wanting to clear her head before she made a final decision. She stood in the parking lot, her arms crossed, watching as the cars drove back and forth. Almost all of them were luxury vehicles. The landscape around the plaza was meticulously kept and not a single pothole marred the lot.

Julie walked out and stood next to Sabina, quiet at first. After a few moments of looking around, Julie turned to her friend and put her hand on her shoulder. "Are you all right?"

Sabina rolled her shoulders, brandishing a smile. "That's a loaded question."

Julie nodded. "You don't have to make the decision. If you lose out on this place, there will be others. But I have a feeling that your hesitation has more to do with the idea that all of this is real; that all of it's actually happening, and that's hard for you to take in. All I can say about that is that if you're truly not ready for this, for whatever reason, then put it on hold; but if you *are* ready, which I think you've been for very long time, then don't let Jonathan and his betrayal affect anything else in your life. What-ever you do, don't let fear hold you back from your dreams."

Sabina took in Julie's words, just as she always had. Julie not only told her the truth, but she was one hell of a motivator as well. Slowly a smile moved across Sabina's lips and her gaze darted to one side, taking in her best friend. "I think you just want me to get out of that apartment so you're not so embarrassed for me."

Julie gritted her teeth and hissed through them, shrugging her shoulders. "Well, maybe just a little." They both laughed and Julie put her arm around Sabina's shoulders. "You know that's not the reason. I've never been embarrassed of you. That's not going to change because you have some tiny sublet filled to the brim with ridiculously expensive furniture. I just want you to be happy. You *deserve* to be happy. You gave up your house for this, so you might as well go all out and make it work."

Sabina looked through the plate-glass window to the gutted concrete-block walls, trying to see beyond the amount of work it would take to restore the space to a viable retail establishment. She clapped her hands together and turned to Julie. "Well, then, let's get this show on the road. If the place needs a total overhaul we need to get started. After all, I can't make a living until I get my business up and running."

Julie and Sabina high-fived each other as they'd done countless times since they were kids. It was their way of getting excited, and also happened to be something that completely embarrassed both of their daughters. They didn't care though.

Sabina walked back into the showroom and grinned at Beverly. "I'll take it. Let me know what you need and let's get this lease signed as soon as possible."

Beverly grinned, motioning toward the door. "Come on, let's go back to my office and sign the paperwork. Did you bring your checkbook?"

Sabina beamed as she followed Beverly out. "Why is that always the last question?"

As she shut the door behind her, Sabina glanced back at the space, excitement rushing through her. This was it, the place she was finally going to claim as her own after more than twenty years' worth of dreams. She wasn't sure if she should be elated or absolutely terrified, but either way she was ready to take that leap of faith. She'd already wasted far too much time.

The leasing process for the space was a bit more complicated than renting an apartment, but it went by pretty quickly since Beverly walked her through each step.

By the time Sabina had signed her name on the last page of the lease, the excitement had overwhelmed her. She took the keys and grinned, giving Beverly a huge hug before turning to Julie, ready to move forward. All she wanted to do was go back to the showroom that she could now call her own and start sketching.

"Personally, I'd just move into the showroom and live there while I used it for business," Julie joked as they walked back to the car. "It's like seven times the size of your apartment, there's even a shower in the bathroom."

"Except for one tiny problem: a certificate of occupancy."

"Details, details," Julie said.

They both laughed as Sabina unlocked the car and they climbed in. They buckled their seat belts and Sabina pulled out of the parking lot and headed back toward the showroom. As she drove, Julie tapped her hands on the dashboard, happier than Sabina had seen her in a while. The tense situation with Zoey had really taken a toll on her, but she seemed to be basking in Sabina's excitement. It felt fantastic to share that kind of energy.

"So, what's next?" Julie asked. "Do you have this all planned out? I know that's probably a stupid question considering you plan out everything, but recently you've been kind of flying by the seat of your pants."

"You think that, but I've had this planned for a long time. Next on the docket, we rebuild. We make that showroom better than anything you've ever seen. You won't even be able to walk in there without wanting to redo everything in your house."

Sabina was pumped, and ready to take on the world. She just hoped that the world was ready for her.

CHAPTER 7

*B*ecause her favorite contractor had a major project cancellation, work on Sabina's showroom started on the following Monday. Within days, Sabina's studio and shop began to take shape. The water and electrical utilities came first. It wasn't the most glamorous part of the renovation, but probably were the most important upgrades. It wasn't just because one needed electricity and water, but because electrical led right into the lighting and the lighting was what would showcase every single thread of fabric, every piece of furniture, and every knob and tassel in the entire showroom. Without the right lighting, nothing would stand out and Sabina would have a very difficult time convincing clients they needed certain pieces to complete a home's transformation.

The first day of construction was quite a letdown, at least to Sabina, who was eager to see the finished product. From the beginning, she told Steve Meade, her contractor, that she would be hands-on with everything. She'd worked with him on several projects for clients and she liked and trusted the lanky Jack-of-all-trades. He'd never let her down and despite her gender, he listened to her ideas and often offered ways to enhance them.

Even if Sabina couldn't wire the building herself, she wanted to be present and she wanted to know how everything worked so if there was ever an issue, she would know what to do. What she didn't take into account was that without a full course in electrical work, it would be hard for the electrician to explain everything to her and get the job done on time. Not to mention the fact that standing around watching other people hang electrical wire was probably one of the more boring things she'd ever witnessed.

Despite the snore-worthy visuals, by the end of the day, the water pipes had been capped and the wiring strung throughout the building. Sabina nervously stood by, and apparently with more enthusiasm than the electricians had ever seen from a client over a lighting installation.

During the next week, Sabina continued her new routine of trying to see the project through from beginning to end. Unfortunately, every step in the process seemed to take forever. So, in an effort to minimize the number of times that the crew had to work around her, slowing things down, she attempted to stay away as much as she possibly could. But at the end of each day, she found herself drawn to the place as though an invisible magnet pulled her to stand there, mesmerized, gazing at the empty, darkened but slowly evolving interior.

After the town inspector came to approve the utilities, Steve and his team really started to move on the project.

Aluminum studs lined the concrete block walls, a tangle of wires hung from the frame of what had once been a suspended ceiling, and drywall dust swirled around their pant legs as they walked through the dimly lit interior, the only light coming from the wall of glass that faced the sidewalk outside. Even though the wiring was finished, most of the electrical service had been shut off to do other projects within the space. Battery-powered lights dispelled the gloom. A few curious rubberneckers glanced through the dirty windows as they passed by, but few stopped. Sabina hoped that would soon change.

By the end of day ten, Sabina was so excited about the transformation that she couldn't stand it. To someone who hadn't seen the project on day one, it would still just look like a grubby construction site. But to Sabina, it was coming along perfectly.

When the last of the workmen packed up their tools to head home for the day, only Steve and Sabina remained. As she looked at the unfinished walls, in her mind she saw her drawings coming to life. Hands on her hips, she turned slowly in circles, surveying the space, her imagination filling in the empty places.

Steve tapped her shoulder. "If that smile gets any bigger, that pretty face of yours will crack in two."

Pretty?

Sabina tried to ignore the nebulous compliment. "I can't help it. I'm happy."

Steve glanced around the space. "You waited a long time for this?"

She nodded.

"It's a great space," Steve said. "It's too bad the former tenants stripped everything they could sell." He leveled his blue eyes at her. "This is costing you way more than it should have."

Sabina cringed. "How much more?"

Steve's mouth twisted into a frown. "Let's just say your cost has outgrown my original estimate by twenty percent."

Her heart sank. "That's big."

Steve nodded and chewed his lip. "Then again, I think I know where I can save you some major bucks on a front counter. Let me see your sketch again."

Sabina pulled her bag around in front of her and shuffled through her portfolio, wishing the former tenant had left at least one flat surface. Steve took the drawing and studied it.

He tapped the paper with his finger nodding. "I picked up an old counter from a B-and-B renovation. All it needs is to be sanded and repainted. I can e-mail you a couple of pictures if you like."

"I like, I like! Crown molding?" she asked hopefully.

Steve nodded dramatically. "Gorgeous. In fact, so good looking, you'll want to sleep with it."

Sabina raised an eyebrow. "With or on?"

Steve's lips quirked upward. Was he actually flirting with her? Then it occurred to her that she now *could* flirt with anyone she liked. The only problem was, she wasn't entirely sure she knew how to do it anymore.

"There's a diner a few doors down. Why don't we grab a sandwich and discuss what the job will entail?" Steve said, handing the sketches back to Sabina.

Butterflies fluttered in her stomach. A date? Was he inviting her out on a date?

No, there was no way. She would be paying Steve thousands and thousands of dollars to construct her shop. A sandwich and a cup of coffee were the least he could toss her way, right?

Sabina realized it didn't really matter why he was asking her out to eat, she had every intention of going with him. He was an incredibly good-looking guy, had a great personality, a thriving business, and as far as she knew, he was single. It wasn't like she was looking for a new relationship, but why shouldn't she enjoy a bite of dinner sitting across from someone who actually seemed to enjoy her company? It had probably been ten years since she had that kind of attention, and even then, Jonathan's efforts felt compulsory at best.

"I'd love to."

Holding the door, Steve waited for Sabina as she gathered her things and pulled out her keys. He stepped back as she locked up for the evening, nerves fluttering in the pit of her stomach. They walked along the sidewalk past a craft store to a small family-owned restaurant. Sabina smiled unabashedly at Steve as she passed by him through the door.

The hostess, looking no more than sixteen, showed them to a table in the corner and handed them a couple of menus. Sabina stared at the bill of fare, but her mind was somewhere else—thinking about how much she liked being in Steve's company. They chatted amiably for a few minutes until the waitress came back and filled their glasses with water and asked if they were ready. Sabina was still no closer to figuring out what she wanted to eat, but she didn't want Steve to know so she ordered the first thing her eyes fell on.

"I'll take the Philly," she said, even though she'd never been a fan of cheese steaks.

Steve closed his menu and handed it to the waitress. "You know what, that sounds great. I'll have the same thing."

The waitress wrote down the order and left the table, though Sabina suddenly wished she'd come back. She had been comfortably alone with Steve dozens of times, but it had always been work-related and on-the-job. This time it felt different. Suddenly, with her new-found single status, it made the situation extremely nerve-wracking. She couldn't remember ever being that nervous dating when she was younger, and she didn't think this meal even qualified as such.

"So, how do you like everything my guys have done so far?" Steve asked.

Sabina took a sip of her water, trying to clear the Sahara Desert that had crawled into the back of her throat.

"It all seems to be coming together perfectly. Well, except for that little snafu back there about it costing me an arm and a leg. But I know you're doing the best you can with what you were given to work with."

Steve shrugged. "We are. And I'll definitely send you pictures of that counter when I get home. I think if we cut a couple of corners that no one will notice, we'll get closer to where you want to be with your budget."

Sabina wrinkled her nose and bit her lip, having had a question on her mind for a long time but never asked. "I know I'm paying you to do this job and it's probably awkward for me to ask this question, but I want you to be honest with me."

Steve frowned. "Okay. What is it?"

"When I came to you with these ideas, with the sketches, did I immediately fall into the category of really difficult client?" She asked the question sincerely, hoping beyond hope that the answer wasn't yes. "And it's okay if you tell me yes, I actually want to know. I work in the business and I know a difficult client when I see one."

Steve smirked and shook his head. "Not at all. I think maybe it's because you're knowledgeable about these things that your requests aren't at all unreasonable. Honestly, I look forward to working with you because of that. You always have everything planned out perfectly; you know what you're looking for and have realistic expectations that help to keep you on budget. So no, you're not a difficult client."

Sabina let out a breath, placing a hand on her throat. "Yay!" They both laughed. Steve's perfect grin sent more butterflies fluttering in her stomach.

He looked around the restaurant, noticing that they were pretty much the only people there.

"So, tell me what's been going on in your life? You're starting your own firm, you look fantastic, you seem happier than I've ever seen you."

Sabina let out a giggle, stopping and glancing around the room, slightly surprised at her preteen reaction. "A lot has been going on." She sobered. "I'm getting a divorce, I moved out of my house and into a little shoebox apartment, and I'm starting this business."

"Wow, a whole new you," Steve replied. "It looks good on you though, seriously."

Sabina placed her hands in her lap, blushing slightly. "Thanks. I'm a work in progress, but I'm feeling pretty positive. So, what's going on with you? Busy with work? Family?" She threw in the family part as little black ops. Although she had no intention of dating anyone, it never hurt to ask.

Steve took in a deep breath and shook his head. "I pretty much just work all the time. I'm divorced ten years now and still single, which isn't a totally bad thing, but I don't really get out much. Working steadily keeps me on my toes and exhausted by the end of the day. You're actually the first woman that I've been out to eat with in probably two years."

Sabina laughed, sitting up straight in her chair. "Well, then, I'm flattered."

Steve leaned forward, a smile quirking his lips and he spoke in the same natural manner as he had with every other conversation they'd had, "I'm glad."

It could've been the atmosphere, it could've been the attention, but it also could have been a man Sabina had known for years, handsome as hell, sweet, and the kind of rugged that she found irresistible, sitting across the table from her that made her palms sweat and her heart beat faster than just a little bit. She tried to shrug it off, she tried to tell herself that it was nothing more than a business meeting, but she had never had a businessman look at her the way Steve did. It made her want to have dinner with him every night for the rest of her life.

But then her body tensed and she felt awkward all over again.

She was a woman who wasn't even officially separated from her husband. Why did she feel so guilty for longing for love when her husband had so blatantly cheated on her—had asked for a divorce and had already moved his mistress to their marital bed? Why was there such a double standard?

Sabina wasn't sure she'd ever know the answer to that.

CHAPTER 8

*W*ith some of her financial problems out of the way, the next item on Sabina's list of things to do was to fill her showroom. To do that, she needed to call suppliers and fabric wholesalers, order outrageous amounts of samples, tassels, curtain ties, and all sorts of fun stuff, and try not to think about the expense she was incurring. It was like going on a Christmas shopping spree, and every present was for her. Still, she'd been very careful about the timing of delivery on the items she ordered so that they wouldn't arrive before the showroom was completed and disrupt the work. She was determined it wouldn't be her who would ever hold them up.

As she chose each item, it became clear to Sabina that she was finally going to have everything she had dreamed of. She'd finally get to do exactly what *she* wanted instead of living her life around Jonathan's and Marisa's schedules. She was especially good at reading a client and anticipating what they wanted, then taking those initial seeds and growing her ideas until they surpassed the client's expectations.

And finally, for the first time in her life, Sabina was getting to call the shots. She was going to get to mold and design her shop the way she wanted it. And yes, that meant she was going to make it or break it, all dependent on her own talent, but she wasn't afraid of that risk. In fact, she liked it. She'd gotten so obsessed with the shop that she didn't even care about being alone in the evenings in the tiny apartment. She was far too busy planning, networking, and creating sketch after sketch of the different ways she could organize her shop to appeal to her potential client base.

Sabina ran the numbers, trying to figure out just how reasonable it would be to have more than two clients a month. The numbers seemed to be a bit more concerning than she had originally thought. Slowly it sank in. Sabina was going to have to do more thorough research about the area. She was going to need to figure out what kind of client would be frequenting the shop most often, and how she could make it as profitable as possible. The entire time she had been envisioning her business, she hadn't given much consideration to walk-in trade. But now that she knew just how hard it was going to be to not only pay the bills, but to make a living—a decent living—off of her company, she wasn't about to discourage walk-in clients at all. She would have to embrace them.

Sabina made a list of everybody she knew. She was going to have to do everything she possibly could to have one heck of a grand opening. She listed all the possible ways to market the event, from press releases and letters to brochures, and everything in between. Then it hit her, she should have a cocktail party. It could be a very hands-on grand opening. There was a good possibility no one would buy anything that night, but it would bring awareness of her store to the highest-profile people she knew. Her bread and butter, the base of her business, had always been referrals, and the best way to get those was to show just how amazing her business was going to be.

Sabina loved the party idea, especially as she got to plan it. She could have champagne, hors d'oeuvres, and maybe even live music. She could already picture a harpist or flutist sitting off to one side, playing soothing music in the background. And as far as the food was concerned, it wasn't even a question. Sabina knew exactly who could take care of catering.

"A party for one hundred? A piece of cake," Julie said on the other end of the phone. "And I'm going to give you the food and the servers for free."

"Oh, you can't do that." Sabina shook her head, and she meant it.

Julie scoffed. "Of course, I can. If I added up the number of catering jobs you've arranged for me over the past ten years, I'd have to offer you free food for a thousand."

Sabina blurted out her defiance immediately. "But you'll need that money for when Zoey has her—"

She stopped herself, and the cold silence that followed reminded her of just what a sore subject Zoey's pregnancy was with her mother. Though fifteen, Sabina still thought of Zoey as a child. Julie's heart had hardened when it came to her daughter. It wasn't that she no longer loved her daughter, but the girl had witnessed first-hand how Julie had struggled as a single mom.

"She should have been more careful," Julie continually muttered. "She should have told me she was sexually active. She should have told me she had a boyfriend." Zoey had never revealed the name of the father of her baby. Had Julie ever asked her daughter the most difficult question a parent could ask? Had Zoey been raped?

"I'm already spreading the word that you're opening the shop," Julie continued, as though Sabina hadn't mentioned the forbidden subject. "I have a lot of clients whose houses could use a refresh."

Sabina calmed her tone and placed her hands in her lap, realizing after she'd already misspoken, that there was no way she could continue to fight Julie about it. She was just going to let her best friend take care of her. "Julie, you are the best."

"No, you are. And you deserve the best."

A smile tugged at Sabina's lips. "Yeah, I do."

Julie laughed loudly. "I like that attitude. It's perfect for you. When's your opening day?"

Sabina pursed her lips, looking up at her calendar. "I hadn't given it a thought. Steve said the renovations would be complete sometime in mid-November."

She heard Julie turning pages—probably in her big work planner. "That does it. How about the Friday before Thanksgiving? People will still be in town and thinking about the holidays and how they wished they'd made their homes look as pretty as possible before Christmas."

Sabina scrunched her brow and slowly shook her head. "No one in their right mind waits until Thanksgiving to think about a holiday home redesign."

"So, you schedule them for January. People will be in the mood to party. Party people like to spend. Let them spend their money on your talents," Julie pointed out.

The more Sabina thought about it, the more she realized that Julie was right. She had set aside more than enough money to make it through until January without any high-profile clients, and the cocktail party could cement that for her. If she was lucky, she could walk into the new year with a full schedule, a calm private life, and a bright future. Not to mention the fact that when you have those kinds of events and everyone is around each other, they tend to book pretty quickly, not wanting to be the odd man out. In high society, dropping your designer's name was almost as normal as name dropping rich friends or powerful people.

"I seriously don't know what I would do without you," Sabina told Julie. "If my business ever becomes successful, I'm going to hire you to market it and become my company spokesperson."

Julie laughed. "You'll get the hang of it. Sometimes it just takes an outside perspective. When it's something so important to you, it's hard to think outside-the-box. You immediately go to the safest options, but sometimes those aren't necessarily worth all the work you have to put into them. With this, you're starting your marketing by offering cocktails and hors d'oeuvres, and then you're letting those rich and powerful people talk each other into setting up appointments with you. Adult peer pressure at its best, and you need to use it to your advantage."

Sabina had zero qualms about doing things exactly as Julie described. Once she had imprinted herself in that society by producing high-quality designs and happy clients, she could then rely on her talent. But until then, she needed to make sure the most influential people on her contact list were going to be at the cocktail party. The future of her company depended on it, and Sabina was ready to make a huge splash into that world.

As she imagined the party in her mind, there was one face that stood out to her; Steve still dressed in jeans and flannel shirt, with that same charming smile. But even in a sea of people, he would look at her as though she was the only person in the room. He had done it over dinner, and Sabina found herself wanting it to happen again and again. In fact, each day when she woke, she found herself excited to go to work, and not just because this was her new shop, but because she knew Steve would be there. It made her feel like a schoolgirl with a silly crush.

Sabina got off the phone with Julie, thanking her half a dozen times, and went straight to work planning and organizing her ideas for the party. She would wait a bit to mail out the invitations, making sure the timeline didn't get pushed back. The last thing she wanted to do was hold a party in a warehouse with six inches of drywall dust and the build half-completed with no display items or stock to see.

Her excitement was palpable, and Sabina found herself doing what she loved the most, designing and planning.

And this time it was all for her.

CHAPTER 9

*S*abina bit her lip as she tapped the keys on her laptop, feeling as though she were pushing the boundaries of her daughter's knowledge of the impending divorce. Because Sabina hadn't gotten a seething phone call or a wild email from Missy claiming mutiny over the unraveling, and less than soap-opera worthy events in the family, she could only assume her daughter still hadn't been told about the divorce. It had irritated Sabina from the beginning, and she felt as though she was lying to her daughter. Even though her last name was still technically Miller, Sabina began using her maiden name for business purposes. Still, she just wanted all of it to be out in the open and over with. Rip the Band-Aid off and be done with it.

Sitting in front of her laptop, she stared at the screen for a moment, mustering her excitement about her new life over the stench of the old and disposed trash of her past. With a forced smile, she cracked her knuckles and finished composing a message for Missy. She would deal with the rest of it later.

To: Marisa Miller

From: Sabina Reigns
Date: October 20

MISSY,

Did you notice the header? I'm using my maiden name for my Design Center. Your Aunt Julie says that with a powerful name like 'Reigns' I'd rule! It does sound a lot more commanding than Miller, doesn't it? And it's not just a name—it's a sentence! (I thought an English major like you would appreciate the pun.)

The contractor has already started work on the shop. I'm going to have a grand opening the Friday before Thanksgiving. Lots of things are going on. I've also pitched for the huge Parkview Manor renovation, too. Keep your fingers crossed for me.

What's happening at school? Tell all.

More news later!

Love you!

Mom

SABINA WASN'T LYING to her daughter. She just wasn't telling her the truth—or rather a part of the whole story. Pressing the send message felt okay. Baby steps. Right? Well, that was a short-lived thought. Before she could even get up from the computer, she received a response from Missy, and it sent her right over the edge.

HEY MOM,

I was just sitting in the library studying when I got your message. Sounds crazy with your business and everything. But what does Dad think about you using your maiden name? I mean, you've been married forever.

Anyway, don't have a lot of time, big exam this week. I've been studying my butt off. Did Dad tell you I have A-s in all of my classes so far? He was pretty stoked about it and got all embarrassing on me. Please don't let him decorate the house in my college colors, I would die.

Will write soon.

Love you,

Missy

SHE BLINKED AT THE SCREEN, trying to keep her irritation at bay. She wasn't sure why she was so angry. There was no doubt in her mind that Jonathan had chickened out on telling Marisa about the separation and impending divorce. But when the innocent words of her baby girl crossed her screen, suddenly Sabina became mother hen. Not only had Jonathan spoken to Missy, but after all these weeks, that swine still hadn't told their daughter about the divorce. Sabina clenched her fists to avoid spewing the news to Missy, but to actually speak to their daughter, hear her voice, and act like everything was fine for Jonathan? She wondered if the girl had even asked her dad about her mother?

Sabina's jaw clenched, her feelings escalating from being angry to livid. What had Jonathan told their daughter? 'Oh, your mom's great, living in a closet on the other side of town while I move in a girl that could be going to college with you right now. Oh, and the nursery for your new brother or sister is great! We used your mother's soul to paint the walls.'

Sabina grabbed her phone from beside her and dialed Jonathan's number, the phone ringing until his nauseating voice echoed through her head. 'I apologize for the inconvenience, but I'm unable to take your call at this—'

She hung up the phone and slammed it down on the table, crossing her arms over her chest. Missy always thought her mother was incapable of using technology for communication purposes, so Sabina figured she would be okay not responding right away. However, Jonathan owed Sabina an explanation.

Closing Missy's email, she clicked the next. It was a message from a client she had finished a job for just before Jonathan dropped his bombshell. Jonathan had called the job a 'cute side gig.' Sabina was the interior designer for the Chateau Noir tasting room. It was beautiful, with rich woods, deep colors, velvet, Persian rugs, and an old school French Noir type of design. It had been a blast to work on.

Opening the emails, Sabina's smile was instantaneous. The owner had sent her pictures of the Grand Re-Opening event. The place was packed and looked so chic Sabina could barely believe she was the one who came up with the design. At first, she doubted herself—that the design was totally out of her comfort zone, but she quickly fell in love with the dark side of romantic décor.

Seeing that message was all she needed to get her mojo back. She texted Jonathan that he needed to call her ASAP and put him out of her mind. She had work to do, and Sabina was not going to let him and his poor parenting skills disrupt her.

* * *

IT TOOK four calls over three days before Jonathan finally got back to her. Sabina even assigned a ringtone to his call so she could deep breathe before pressing the call icon. But, when that ringtone finally sounded, she didn't bother with pleasantries.

"Why haven't you told Marisa about our divorce?"

Jonathan didn't answer right away. Caught! Oddly enough, instead of excuses he surprised her. "Technically, we're only separated."

Yes. And not even legally.

Sabina kept telling herself over and over to stay calm. "Well, we *are* getting divorced."

Again, silence. "Nothing's final until—"

Sabina cut him off. "Don't you dare tell me you're having second thoughts about this."

"Of course not. It's just—look, I'm very busy," he said, his tone thick with frustration.

It was a tone that was second nature to him, and all too familiar to her. He hated being pressed, and he hated even more being told he wasn't living up to standard. Of course, Sabina didn't *tell* him that per se, but the implication in her words brought a world of defensive guilt down on his shoulders.

"I don't care how busy you are. You agreed to tell Marisa—"

He huffed angrily. "I will, but I don't want to disrupt her schoolwork. The first semester is always the hardest. The adjustment and all."

Her eyes rolled so far back in her head, Sabina nearly died. "And how adjusted do you think she'll feel when she comes home for Thanksgiving and finds your pregnant little Pop-Tart in our bedroom?"

He snapped back, his voice already sounding as though his head was slow to catch up with the words. "Don't talk about Courtney that way. She's the mother of my child."

Sabina's mouth dropped open slowly and her brow furrowed, all that motivating self-talk instantly gagged her. "So am I and look at the respect you've given me over the years."

Stop, Stop, STOP! She yelled at herself and yelled at Jonathan at the same time. Her blood pressure shot into the stratosphere, the palm of her free hand stung from the tips of her nails digging into her flesh, and she experienced a rush of anger, anxiety, and hurt violently vibrating through her chest. Sabina leaned to the side, her eyes shifting out the door of her half-finished office, making sure there weren't any unsuspecting crew members nearby. They definitely would think an exorcism was going on inside.

Sabina swallowed a long breath, rolled her shoulders, and

cracked her neck to calm herself. Though, she had to admit, it was futile at best.

"I don't like keeping the truth from her, Jonathan. It's a lie of omission, but a lie, nonetheless. And unless you want her to hear it from an outside source—"

He scoffed. "Are you threatening me?"

Seriously, Sabina didn't know how her eyes would even focus after this conversation. It was like he knew all the possible things he could say to get her rolling them. "No, I'm just pointing out that we're not her only contacts in the area. She e-mails Julie, Zoey, and God only knows how many other people here."

He was silent again, this time because he knew that Sabina was right. He knew that he could escape Missy's anger in a lot of ways, but if she heard about their divorce from someone else, she would unload on him for sure. And rightly so.

"I see your point. All right, I'll tell her."

Sabina put one clenched fist up in the air and shook it. "Thank you, sheesh. Good-bye."

You rat!

Sure, the dig was spoken in her head, but it felt good all the same so she figured, with the call ended, it would feel even better to say out loud.

"Rat," she growled. "Ratty-rat-rat!"

With a smirk on her lips, Sabina chortled at the childish satisfaction it brought her. Steve's head popped around the corner, making Sabina jump. He entered slowly, a hammer in hand, taking careful steps as his eyes shifted all around the floor. Sabina sucked in a breath, leaning to one side, trying to figure out what exactly he was stalking in her office. "Steve?"

He put his finger to his lips and swiftly ducked down, looking under a crate. With pursed lips, he stood up, scratching the top of his head. "Well, dang."

"What are you looking for?" she asked, slightly amused at his serious expression.

His eyes shifted over to her. "The rat."

Sabina blinked at him for a moment before bursting into laughter. He looked at her, clearly confused. She stood up and walked over to him, unable to stop her laughter. She patted his broad, strong chest and shook her head.

"Oh, man. Sweetie, if you're looking for the rat I was talking about, you're gonna have to travel to a law firm in Linden Oaks."

"Oh," he said and smirked with embarrassment. "So, you were calling someone a rat, not letting me know you *had* a rat in here."

Sabina's laughter had simmered enough to where she could talk through the giggle. "I'm sorry. But thank you so much for being ready to tackle the monster with your hammer and sheer will."

He smiled that gorgeous, perfect smile as he ran his dusty hand through his hair. His biceps bulged beneath his rolled-up sleeves. Sabina's hand was still on his chest and their eyes met as his hand fell to hers. There was a silence in the room but their gazes communicated loudly to each other.

Sabina felt a pull in her chest she hadn't felt in years. That initial attraction, the excitement behind it, the blazing passion hidden beneath rugged good looks and the perfect smile. Her body slowly leaned toward his. Just as she began to close her eyes, with no real thoughts in her mind, and for the scent of his skin making her feel giddy, someone in the other room dropped something, sending a loud clanging reverberation through the entire showroom.

Sabina pulled her hand back, clearing her throat. Steve awkwardly looked back and forth and pointed out the door. "I should—"

"Yeah," she said and nodded, putting her hands behind her back as she walked back to the desk.

As soon as he cleared her sight, she rolled her eyes and leaned back, covering her face. Sabina knew she was not meant for the dating world after such a long absence, but at the same time,

Steve made her feel like her feet couldn't possibly touch the ground anytime she was around him. It wasn't planned or even really wanted, but she knew she had a serious crush going. A crush that seemed nearly impossible.

Rebound relationships seldom lasted, and yet Sabina could dream.

CHAPTER 10

"Can you believe it," Julie said, her nose wrinkled. "Jonathan actually called and asked me to cater his Thanksgiving dinner. Does Courtney not have the most basic cooking skills?"

Slumped on the couch, Sabina grabbed a handful of popcorn from the bowl in her lap and shoved it in her mouth. Julie sat on the floor in front of her, a snack buffet stretched out on Sabina's thirteen hundred-dollar antique Nasiri Mahal rug that she had triumphantly snagged for significantly less from an old client who had gotten tired of the color. Sabina had stashed it in her office, rolled up in the corner, waiting for just the right place and time to use it. It was one of the first things she thought about when she found out she would be thrown out of her own place. It gave her comfort knowing it never saw the light of day during her marriage.

"I've never seen her cook," Sabina replied with her mouth full. "Of course, I've never really seen her do anything but scowl and prance."

Julie snorted. "Well, we know the one thing she apparently does well."

Sabina threw a piece of popcorn at her friend. "Don't be vulgar. You're talking about the mother of my child's sister or brother."

Julie shook her head, looking back at me. "Oh, come on, nobody's *that* charitable."

Sabina suppressed a smile. "Who's being charitable? I'm looking out for myself. I don't intend to badmouth Jonathan or Courtney in front of Marisa, and I figure I'd better start practicing in advance. We all know someone who *is* that person. The one that talks crap to their kids about the other parent. Shoot, remember Helena from that party we took Marisa and Zoey to about five years ago? She talked smack constantly and they weren't divorced or even separated."

Julie laughed, pressing her fingers to her lips, trying not to spit out her soda. She nodded and finally swallowed. "Yes! And you know they'll be the ones that are together for like seventy years."

Sabina giggled. "They'll both live so long because they're too stubborn to die first. So, they'll hobble around bickering, fighting, and making each other miserable."

"Just like my parents," Julie said and groaned. "I think I've experienced enough torture in relationships that I would rather not be around it for the rest of my life."

Sabina nodded hard. "Agreed."

Julie tossed back some chocolate-covered raisins and turned, leaning her shoulder against the couch next to Sabina. "So, what are you doing for Thanksgiving?"

Sabina shrugged, her eyes glued to the movie in front of her, but her mind lacking any sort of attention for the romantic comedy they had chosen for their girls night in—not that it was night *yet*. Julie had no jobs booked for the weekend and the friends had spent the morning window shopping since Sabina needed to hold onto every nickel she could until she had a steady income. "I haven't thought that far ahead. I just want to get through the grand opening."

Julie reached up and slapped Sabina's knee. "You better get on that. It's only a week and a half away. Will you have Marisa or will Jonathan?"

Sabina let out a long painful sigh. "As Jonathan is so quick to point out, she's of legal age. She can choose whomever she wants to be with."

"But you'd like it to, be you?" Julie asked.

Sabina sat up, nodding. "Of course, who wouldn't? How small do turkeys come? I can't cook a twenty-pounder for just the two of us."

Julie looked bewildered at the thought. "Not unless you're terribly fond of leftovers and have the space to store them."

Reaching over, Sabina grabbed her phone. "I guess I can make a reservation at a restaurant. I can always cancel."

Julie shuddered. "No, you will not spend your first Thanksgiving of freedom, with or without your eighteen-year-old daughter, in some mediocre restaurant serving subpar turkey, listening to the elevator version of Christmas tunes over a loudspeaker. You can have Thanksgiving with us. Not that it will be much better, the way things have been going between Zoey and me."

Sabina grimaced, hating how much toil and drama Julie had been going through. At the same time though, she was glad that her best friend had finally reached the point where she could even mention the situation out loud. "She still won't tell you the baby's father's name?"

Julie shook her head, her simmering gaze focused off in the distance. Sabina knew Julie was struggling and she was absolutely there for her, but she knew there wasn't much she could say to make her feel better. She wished Julie would come to peace with it and not be so at odds with her daughter. But Sabina looked at life a

69

little differently than Julie. When you couldn't change something, you did your best to enjoy the positives of it. Julie had a right to feel bitter and disappointed, but Sabina feared it would affect everything in Julie's life for a very long time if she couldn't get past it.

Knowing there was nothing she could do, and with the silence taking a toll on both of them, Sabina changed the subject.

"I want to do something nice for Steve and his crew."

Julie's brows lifted and she took in a deep breath, pulling herself back to the room. "Throw them a lunch. Subs, chips, pop. Might cost you fifty bucks or so, but the goodwill is worth a million."

Sabina snapped her fingers, grabbing her notebook to jot it down. "That's a great idea. Steve and the guys have been working their butts off, trying to help me achieve my vision within my limited budget."

Julie's eyebrows went up and she leaned forward, resting her chin on her arm. "Uh, Steve? What happened to *the contractor?*"

"What? I shouldn't call him by his name?" Sabina knew better than to look up at that moment, knowing Julie was waiting for any sign of weakness.

"No, you can call him whatever you like. It's not *what* you called him, it's the *way* you said it. Your cheeks got all rosy, you struggled to keep that glimmer out of your Steve-loving eyes."

Sabina could feel a blush warming her cheeks, and she immediately slapped Julie's hand. "I did not."

"Oh, yes you did, and you do it every time," Julie replied, sitting up excitedly on her knees. "Now, don't rush into anything. Take it slow, enjoy this new era in your life, touch a muscle or two, watch him split wood in the pouring rain, shirtless—you know, the usual stuff of Hallmark movies."

Sabina tried not to laugh but she couldn't help it. "You *do* realize this is real life, not a steamy romance novel, right? And my contractor is just that, not a lumberjack in the middle of the woods, which are pretty non-existent nearby, I might add. So, you'll have to play out your longing for a movie happy ending somewhere else. Besides, my relationship with Steve is strictly professional."

"Of course, it is," Julie said and nodded with a serious expression. Slowly her lips curled into a nefarious grin. "So, how do we make sure it *does* become personal?"

Sabina kicked her legs out from underneath her and stood, taking the bowl to the kitchen, a few feet away. "You're too much, Julie. Always seeing things that aren't actually there."

Julie slunk back, grabbing her bowl and holding a few pieces in her hand. "I prefer to think I'm faster on the uptake than you. I've been single a hell of a lot longer, and you know I've always been more aware of the men around us. I've seen the way that lumberjack contractor looks at you."

Sabina stood in front of Julie, her arms folded across her chest. "No, you *imagined* the way he looks at me."

Sabina fought the idea, but she knew damn well that just the week before when chasing 'rats' in her office, she and Steve had almost shared a kiss. She also knew that if she kissed him, she might never stop had run through her mind more than once. Then there was the ogling, the deep sighs, the flushed cheeks, and the giggles. But it was all beside the point. Sabina was single and *old*. Steve was close in age but extremely attractive. And he definitely looked way younger than he actually was. Didn't he?

Julie continued to tease Sabina until she finally threw her arms up and headed back to the bedroom to change. Julie furrowed her brow. "Where are you going?"

Sabina pulled on a pair of jeans and a blue-and-white striped blouse, scraping her hair back at the nape of her neck. "I still have an hour before Steve and the crew call it quits for the weekend to get an update on where we are. The party is just a week away. I won't be gone more than an hour, tops. Just stay here and wait for me."

Julie pulled herself up on the couch and followed Sabina with a stare. "Tell *Steve* I said hi. Oh wait, that's right, he only wants greetings and salutations from the boss lady."

Sabina grabbed her purse, pausing at the door before rolling her eyes and walking out. She had to admit, no matter how ridiculous the thought of her and Steve together was, it was still right there at the front of her mind. As she drove, just for a moment, Sabina indulged herself, letting the notion run wild in her mind.

As she pulled up to the shop, she found the front door propped open and a couple of guys carrying in crates. It looked like shelving parts. A thick layer of dust covered the floor and she could see white particles billowing in the light from the new fixtures above. She grabbed her bag, realizing it was a 'messy day' at the renovation site. As she walked up, she stopped, helping one of the crew carry in a box.

She stumbled back as she tripped over the door frame, feeling a strong hand push against her back to keep her from stumbling. Sabina moved to the side and set the box down, dusting off her hands. There was Steve, his hand still hovering just above her body, smiling at her.

"Putting the boss to work. You're stronger than I thought. Shall we just have you move the rest of the crates in?"

Sabina scoffed as she tied a bandanna around her head. "Yeah, right. I might just struggle with one and trip again, and then you guys would have to scoop me up off the floor."

Steve rubbed a thumb over the bridge of her nose. "You look incredibly cute covered in drywall dust."

Sabina scrunched her forehead. "Cute? I think the last time someone called me cute I was five-years-old."

Steve laughed, putting his arm across his waist and bowing slightly. "Sorry about that. Beautiful. I meant, beautiful."

Sabina's heart was thudding as she looked up into his deep blue eyes. He lowered his head and she didn't waste a moment, closing her eyes as his lips touched gently down on hers. A small whimper bubbled in her throat as she stepped closer, pressing her body against his. As the magic unfolded, wrapping them together, Sabina realized she hadn't felt even a stirring of passion from a kiss in a long time. More than that, Steve was the first man she'd kissed other than her husband in over twenty years.

That old married side of her felt as though she should go running from the place, throw in the towel on her business, go into the Witness Protection Program, hide from her shame, and immediately confess her transgressions to her husband. But wait, she didn't have one, and he had already taken his transgressions to the ultimate level.

No, Sabina stayed there in Steve's arms, knowing full well she deserved to be happy, even if it was just for a little while. She wasn't doing anything wrong. She was allowed to kiss whomever she wanted. There were no more ties to the past or ties to her soon-to-be-ex, just ties to her happiness and well-being from that point on.

That one kiss reminded Sabina that she was a woman, beautiful and powerful, and even the lumberjack thought so.

CHAPTER 11

$\mathcal{T}$he alarm rang out loud and clear at six-fifteen, but Sabina was already awake, lying in bed trying to quell the rolling waves of nerves within her. Though she'd felt exhausted, she hadn't slept much. The previous few days had been absolutely crazy as the work crew labored to make sure the showroom, though not completed, was party-ready. Sabina had decided they'd only put out her best pieces, and once painted, the counter Steve had supplied was perfect and would make a great buffet for the food and as a bar. When she'd left the evening before the place looked nearly perfect, but there were enough small tasks still undone that would keep Sabina busy for a good part of the day.

As she pulled herself out of the bed, she glanced over at the picture of her daughter, sitting on the nightstand. She was so excited and nervous about the party that night but was equally nervous that Marisa would be returning home for Thanksgiving the next week. Still, Sabina dreaded the holiday. Thanksgiving was supposed to be a time to celebrate, but she knew that instead of smiles and laughter, there'd be a lot of shouting, hard feelings, and tears. She was glad she'd decided to have the grand opening the week before Thanksgiving so the inevitable drama of both events wouldn't be happening all at once.

Not only would Marisa find out about the divorce, but she'd be blindsided by having to meet the woman destined to be her stepmother, as well as finding out she was to become a big sister. The whole situation would be dramatic and Sabina was furious with Jonathan because he still hadn't told Marisa. Sabina loved her daughter, but she would be the first one to admit that the girl was a bit of a drama queen. She often let her attitude get the best of her, and usually directing her ire at Sabina. Marisa was a daddy's girl and always had been.

Sabina tried to put it out of her mind, showering, dressing, and preparing to leave. She decided to take her party clothes with her so she could change later, just in case the showroom needed more attention. Steve had promised to drop by to make sure everything would sparkle, but as much as she trusted him, Sabina wasn't sure his—or anyone else's—efforts would live up to her standards.

The thought gave her a case of the guilts. Was she that much of a control freak? With so much on her mind, Sabina tucked the thought away figuring she would have time to ponder her short-comings later—much later. Still, she was grateful he'd offered to help, both for emotional support and because she was short-handed and couldn't afford to hire anyone to pitch in at the last minute.

As Sabina filled her travel mug with coffee, her phone pinged. A text from Julie.

Deep breaths. Every time you get stressed, think about lumberjacks.

Sabina allowed herself a smile and sent Julie a smiley face emoji before tucking her phone into her bag. Throwing her garment bag over her arm, she grabbed her coffee and headed out the door. There wouldn't be anybody at the shop when she arrived, as the sun had barely come up, but she wanted that little bit of time by herself in the emptiness of her new place to go over everything she needed to do for the day and make a plan.

Traffic was light at that time of the morning, and she was at her shop in half the time it normally took. Walking inside, waves of lavender-scented oils, fresh carpets, and a hint of lemon polish from the night before wafted over her. She nodded approvingly, knowing it was important from the moment her clients walked through the doors that their senses were filled with positivity.

Alone in her shop, Sabina took a moment to study her surroundings. During the construction, she'd seldom been alone in the place. It had taken all hands to get the job finished in time. Standing in the center of the showroom, with the closed shopping center silent, Sabina considered how much she'd accomplished in two months. Sure, the shop's transformation had taken a boatload of money, but the depths of her talent would be revealed once she began to pick up clients. She had taken that big step—something she wouldn't have had the courage to even consider if Jonathan hadn't shattered her quiet, complacent rut.

Oddly enough, she felt grateful to the cad. Traumatic as the past few months had been, it was beginning to look like divorce might be best for everyone. Of course, Missy wouldn't understand that, not until she was older, but it wasn't about Missy, it was about Sabina.

The door opened behind her and, startled, Sabina turned to find a delivery guy standing before her with the clipboard. "I'm looking for Sabina Reigns."

Sabina let out a breath and crossed the floor to meet him. "That's me."

He held out the paperwork. "I've got a truckload of flowers for you. If you could sign here."

Sabina scratched her reclaimed name across the line and propped open the door. "Do you need help?"

The delivery guy tucked the clipboard beneath his arm and

shook his head. "No, I brought a guy with me. Where do you want them?"

Sabina grinned, pointing at the counter. "You can just line them up there."

He nodded and left the shop.

The day had begun. From that point on, there wouldn't be a moment of peace until the party was over. And yet, at the end of the day, when everyone had gone home, she still wouldn't know if she had succeeded. Only time—and a ringing phone with potential clients asking about her availability to transform their homes—would tell.

* * *

DRESSED AND READY, Sabina glanced at the clock above her desk and bit her lip. With less than an hour before showtime, Julie and the catering crew had yet to show up. Nor had the vintner. Sabina found herself rubbing the empty spot on her left ring finger where, until recently, a band of gold had resided. Sabina had never hosted a party without Jonathan, not that he contributed more than opening wine bottles and mixing drinks. Happily, though, she didn't feel nearly as abandoned as she'd anticipated.

The bell over the shop door rang and Sabina leapt from her chair, smashing her right knee into the open desk drawer. With a yelp of pain, she groped at her leg, finding a gaping tear in her pantyhose. Why in hell was she was even wearing the damn things in the first place?

"Could anything else go wrong?" she muttered, as she limped out of her office.

Instead of the wine or food crew, a well-dressed young man in a three-piece suit, neatly trimmed brown hair, and a smile stood in front of the service counter, taking in the well-appointed showroom. He held a business-sized envelope in one hand, the other was poised over the brass counter bell.

"Can I help you?"

He held out his hand to shake hers. "Hi, remember me? Todd Foreman. We met at Parkview Manor back in early September."

"Vaguely," Sabina admitted, but then the memory came back with a jolt. Charles Patterson's arrogant little toady. "Why are you here?" she asked suspiciously.

"I'm your new assistant."

Sabina blinked. "Excuse me?"

His hand dropped back down to his side. "When we first met I didn't have an opportunity to tell you my credentials. I graduated from your alma mater—Syracuse University. I've got three years of interior design experience and have a working knowledge of antiques, fabrics, vintage linens, and—"

Sabina lifted her brow. "And I'm not hiring."

Todd took it in stride, almost as though he had expected Sabina's initial reaction. He gave her a sweet smile and took a calming breath. "You need me. You recently completed the Chateau Noir Tasting Room, are just about to open Sabina Reigns Interior Designs and landed the coveted Parkview Manor renovation, something every designer in Western New York has been after."

"And I'm still not hiring," Sabina replied, stopping mid-turn to look back at him. "Wait, did you just say I landed the Parkview Manor Renovation?"

Todd grinned. "I spoke with the caretaker this morning. She loved your innovation and big ideas. She's going to call you after Thanksgiving, and that's why you need me."

Sabina shook her head, her mind clouded by so much information at once. "While I appreciate the tip, I still can't hire you."

The young man stood back, hands on hips, and actually pouted. "You know I *could* call the New York Department of Labor and report you."

Sabina furrowed her brow. "What for?"

"Discrimination." Todd straightened to the point of rigidity. "I'm gay."

Again Sabina blinked. Then she laughed. "Threatening a potential employer doesn't make a good first impression."

Todd brightened. "*Potential* employer. See, you're already considering me, and you haven't even looked at my impressive resume."

He handed Sabina the envelope. She sighed and made her way around the counter. Shuffling in the drawers, she found the letter opener at the back and slit the envelope, all while staring at Todd, unamused. She skimmed the neat text. "What happened to your job with Charles Patterson?"

Todd's mouth tightened. "We weren't a good fit and I decided to pursue other employment."

A white panel truck with Connoisseur Catering stenciled on the side pulled up out front.

Sabina handed Todd his resume and moved toward the door. "I'm sorry, Todd. As much as I need an assistant, I'm just not in a position to hire one right now."

Instead of getting angry, Todd smiled, putting the envelope back on the counter, giving it a small pat. "You'll change your mind. Keep my resume on the top of the pile because when the time comes, it's me that you'll choose."

Sabina tried but failed to suppress a smile, finding his personality amusing. "I'll do that."

Todd stepped outside and held the plate glass door open for Julie, who held a huge crystal punch bowl. "Sorry I'm late. There was an accident on the expressway. There's something absolutely gooey all over the road."

She set the bowl on the counter and headed back to the truck.

Sabina hobbled to the door just in time to intercept Julie's very pregnant teenage daughter, Zoey, carrying a large cardboard carton. "Here, let me help you with that."

"Thanks," the girl panted before heading back out the door.

Sabina deposited the heavy box on the counter and threw a look over her shoulder. The truck had two rows of seats and no one else had emerged from the back. Julie had promised three servers.

Julie struggled through the door, carrying a collapsed table and a sheaf of linens tossed over one shoulder.

"Where are Diane and Mary?" Sabina asked, grabbing the front end of the table and helping Julie carry it to the side of the showroom.

"Fired," Julie puffed. "They were fleecing me, taking my supplies and catering their own jobs on the side. I couldn't find anyone to fill in, so it's just Zoey and me tonight. We can manage."

Sabina's stomach began to churn almost instantly. "But I'm expecting over a hundred guests—"

"You worry too much." Julie set up the table and threw out the tablecloth so it billowed over, and then neatly settled on the table. "Hand me that punch bowl, will you?"

Knee still smarting, Sabina crossed the room, grunting as she lifted the bowl, and shuffled back over, praying the entire time that she didn't drop the thing—or throw out her back.

"Thanks," Julie replied, taking the bowl and looking suspiciously down at Sabina's knee. "Did you know you've got a huge hole in your pantyhose?"

Sabina stared at her, emotionless. "I noticed."

"Help!" came a small voice.

Sabina did a limping hop over to the door to intercept Zoey, who struggled with a bulky hamper of food. Sabina shook her head, reaching for it. "Let me take that."

"She can do it," Julie said coldly.

Sabina glanced over her shoulder. "But Julie, surely she shouldn't be hefting that kind of weight in her condit—"

Zoey's cheeks flushed as her gaze shifted to her mother. Zoey looked all of twelve, not fifteen. "I got it. Thanks anyway, Aunt Sabina."

Sabina pretended to look around behind the counter, waiting for the awkward moment to subside. It didn't. And the fact that the girl still refused to name the father of her baby had driven an even deeper wedge between mother and daughter.

Despite her youth, Zoey had been helping her mother for years, and ably took over the set-up as Julie finished unpacking the truck. Sabina did what she could to help, annoyed that she risked a shimmering new cocktail dress that had *not* come off Talbot's sale rack as she'd hoped.

Julie climbed back into the truck, sliding behind the steering wheel and took off to park just as the Chateau Noir Wine Company van pulled up to the door. The engine died and the emergency flashers came to life. Divinely handsome, forty-something Robert Martin rounded the van and opened the back. "Sorry I'm late. Accident on—"

"The expressway. Yes, I heard." Sabina glanced at her watch. Less than thirty minutes and counting. "Is Annette joining you?"

"Not tonight. But I'm okay," Robert grunted as he picked up a crate.

Ordinarily, she'd rejoice in the absence of Robert's jealous wife, but now they were short-staffed on the wine *and* catering front. "Can I help you set up?"

"No need. I'll be done in a jiffy." Robert flashed a glowing smile, withdrew a scuffed wooden wedge from inside the van, and propped the showroom's door open. Then he flexed his muscles as he piled cases of wine and champagne onto a dolly and wheeled them inside.

Julie returned from the parking lot, looking rather glum, so Sabina made hasty introductions to keep Julie from unleashing her attitude on poor Robert, then stood back to watch the showroom's elegant living room set transform into an upscale dining salon.

True to his word, in minutes, Robert had set up and filled ice buckets, assembled the glassware and napkins, and changed into a tux jacket, looking like the groom on top of a wedding cake. Sabina glanced down at the hose hanging in tatters at her knee. Did she have time to make it to the drug store to buy a new pair? Probably not. She would just have to go with bare legs, wishing she had more of a tan.

The bell over the door rang again and Sabina tensed, ready to greet her first guest. Instead of someone of means, ready to invite Sabina into their home to transform it, a smiling Todd Foreman stood in the doorway, holding four packages of pantyhose. "I wasn't sure about the size, so I got an assortment. I chose black because they'd go so well with that little number you're wearing."

Sabina let out an exaggerated breath, dropping her arms low and shuffling over to Todd. "Thank goodness! You've saved the day."

Todd looked smug. "I told you—you need me."

"You're absolutely right," Sabina said, stopping in her tracks. Slowly her mouth curved into a smile and she triumphantly turned around. "Now, what are you better at? Serving wine or hors d'oeuvres?"

CHAPTER 12

"*T*his wasn't what I had in mind," Todd growled just loud enough for Sabina to hear. He offered her a crab-meat *canapé*. True, the white server's jacket didn't go well with his pinstriped, wool trousers, but he did look kind of cute in a Connoisseur Catering chef's hat.

Sabina selected a mini spinach quiche instead, settling it on a buff-colored cocktail napkin. "Smile, sweetie. You're gainfully employed—if only for the evening."

Todd rolled his eyes and stepped away, but he did quickly don a smile as he asked one of the guests to try a *canapé*. So far everything was running smoothly. The champagne flowed, brochures and business cards had been disappearing from the front counter, and all the guests—mostly former clients—seemed relaxed with happy, mellow conversations bountiful.

It seemed like most of the people Sabina ever worked with or loved—except for Jonathan and Marisa—had attended. She waved a quick hello to Toby Wallace, her accountant. As he nodded and moved toward a seat in the farmhouse living room set, Sabina focused her vision on a tall man standing on the other side of the room. It was Steve, looking suave, handsome, and any

83

other adjective that could describe a hunka hunka burning love. He threw Sabina a kiss, his smile as bright as a million-watt light bulb. Blushing slightly, she sidled past acquaintances, friends, former co-workers, and clients, drinking in their praise and good wishes, to join him.

Steve grabbed her hand, gave her a quick kiss on the lips, and settled right into things as though he had always belonged right there by her side. Sabina gave him a quick steamy look, glad that they had moved past the awkward almost kiss, to the teasing lustful back and forth. "I hope that's a preview of what's to come."

He grinned and the sound of his voice caused a pleasant tingling in Sabina's chest. "Absolutely."

Sabina glanced around at the crowd. "Have your ears been burning, I've been singing your praises as the genius who brought my designs to life."

"I may have handed out a few of my own business cards," Steve admitted.

Julie popped into her line of sight, giving Sabina a thumbs-up with a cheesy smile as she brought out another platter of hot *hors d'oeuvres* from the tiny kitchen in the back.

The front door opened with a jangle. Sabina turned, her smile faltering as Charles Patterson entered the showroom. The party wasn't invitation-only, and a few people passing by with a nose for free food and drink had already crashed, but Sabina had never expected Patterson to show.

Todd looked up from his tray and spied Patterson, his face immediately flushing. With an abrupt about-face, he stalked off toward the kitchen, but Patterson's voice stopped him. "Todd, is that really you?"

Heads turned, and the murmur of voices quieted.

"Excuse me," Sabina told Steve.

Patterson, followed by three pretty women, made a beeline for Todd. He took in Todd's chef hat and the near-empty tray he held. "I see you've finally found work that suits your skills," he said dryly.

Titters of laughter erupted from Patterson's entourage. He always did like his *protégés* young and attractive. The better to exploit them—in every way possible.

Sabina stepped forward. "Todd very graciously offered to help. Generosity is just one of his many attributes."

Todd managed a smile but continued on his course for the kitchenette.

Patterson turned to Sabina, a look of disdain coloring his face as his eyes rolled from her feet to the top of her head, inspecting every crease and hair. "You look lovely, Sabrina. New dress? I heard you were driven to the poor house after your husband left you."

Sabina swallowed down the bile Patterson's presence always inspired in her. That he'd called her by the wrong name was just another of his tactics to undermine her confidence. "Now, now, Charles, play nice. My split with Jonathan was entirely amicable and mutually agreed upon. I am not in financial difficulty. Otherwise, how could I open this splendid showroom?"

Patterson rolled his eyes to the left. "Yes, but darling, you're located in a strip mall."

Sabina kept her cool as a small smirk crossed her lips. She knew that if he was insulting her, then he felt threatened by her. "The plaza is a thriving retail complex. I expect I'll do very well here."

Patterson waved a hand. "If you say so. What does one have to do to get offered a drink around here?"

"Robert would be more than happy to pour you some wine." Steeling herself, Sabina took Patterson's arm and steered him to the bar. "Robert, please take special care of my dear friend, Charles."

Robert nodded and smiled. "Champagne?"

Sabina abandoned Patterson and paused to tidy the brochures on the counter.

"A tad sweet, isn't it?" she heard Patterson say. "Then again, it really isn't Champagne if it doesn't come from that region in France, eh?"

Sabina's jaw ached from clenching it. Across the way, she saw Julie give Patterson a narrow-eyed glare. Parties like this were important for her, too, as it was an advertisement for her catering abilities. She wasn't going to fare well with someone picking apart every bit of her work, especially not in front of the type of people that could easily become her clients.

Sabina waited until she caught Julie's eye and winked at her before heading for the kitchenette, stopping along the way to encourage her guests to enjoy themselves.

Todd poked his head around a cabinet. "What is *he* doing here?" he hissed.

Sabina's lip curled as she stacked a couple of empty trays. "Probably trying to steal my clients."

"Better tell Julie to count her silverware, too," Todd remarked.

Sabina lifted her brow and glanced over at the food, waiting to be served. "Are you going to hide here for the rest of the evening?"

Todd exhaled a deep breath. "Patterson is enough to drive a gay man straight. But then I understand even you've had your own unpleasant experiences with him."

Sabina shuddered at the thought. It wasn't a secret. She *had* been a *protégé* of Charles Patterson some twenty years before. Despite the shabby treatment he was famous for dishing out to his employees, crushing their spirits and claiming their innovative ideas and designs as his own, he remained the darling of Pittsford/Mendon society. Sabina despised him.

"And you *do* need me," Todd said, changing the subject. "There are at least three dowagers out there plotting to hire you, and you can't handle them plus the Parkview renovation without alienating someone."

Sabina let out a sigh, knowing he was right, but having no real choice at that moment. "Between opening the shop and paying for this little soirée, I'm in hock up to my eyebrows," she muttered.

Todd sniffed. "A mere cash-flow interruption. I'll give you a week of my services for free. If at the end of that time you decide you can live without me, I'll go without a backward glance."

Sabina shook her head, her eyes glued on Patterson. "That would be grossly unfair to you. I simply can't afford to hire you."

"Okay, but if you like my work, how about you write me a terrific reference." Todd wiggled his eyebrows and beamed.

Sabina thought about the office chores that needed to be attended to and wavered. Copying, stuffing envelopes and mailing them and follow-up phone calls to clients were only a few of the tasks that needed to be completed over the next few days. Feeling the weight of the world on her shoulders, in addition to her relatively disastrous personal life, Sabina gave in.

"Okay, Todd. It's a deal."

A scowling Zoey bustled into the kitchenette carrying two empty hors d'oeuvres trays. "Boy—those three skinny chicks sure can eat." She grabbed a potholder and opened the oven door. The scent of figs wrapped in Prosciutto wafted over them. "Hey, Todd, can you help me arrange these on a platter?"

Todd grunted in a high pitch, turning with a wave of his hand. "At least someone appreciates my artistic sensibilities, even if the results are only destined for 'Charlie's Angels' and their robust appetites."

Sabina allowed herself a smile before breathing deeply to calm her rattled nerves before heading out to the party once again. With only another hour to go, she could then close the door, go back to her little apartment, change into sweats, and kick back with a huge glass of wine. The mere thought of it beckoned to her, and she struggled to lift her feet as she walked. Shuffling would have been so much more reasonable at that point.

The bell over the door jingled once again. Another late comer? She cast a glance over her shoulder and nearly gave herself a case of whiplash. Standing framed in the doorway, dressed in a down jacket, boots, and scarf, with her hair artfully windblown, was her daughter, Marisa.

"Missy!" Julie called, abandoning her post behind the hors d'oeuvres table. She threw her arms around Marisa, cooing over her like she was her long-lost child, while Zoey glowered from across the room.

Marisa searched the crowd beyond Julie, still holding onto the handle of her little black suitcase.

Sabina hurried across the room. "Missy, what are you doing here? You're not due in until next Wednesday."

She gave her daughter a much-needed hug, taking in the familiarity of her pear body spray and freshly washed locks.

Marisa grunted as Sabina squeezed her hard. "You didn't think I'd miss your opening, did you?"

There was a hint of panic in Sabina's stomach as she pulled back. "Looks like you came straight from the airport."

Marisa propped up her suitcase and shook out the wrinkles in her coat. "I did."

Sabina searched her daughter's happy, glowing face. She still had no clue about the impending demise of her parents' marriage. "Did your Dad know you were coming?"

"No." She searched the crowd again. "Where is he? He didn't stiff you to work late again, did he?"

For a moment Sabina wasn't sure what to say. "I didn't expect him to come."

She frowned. "That's not like Dad."

Sabina twisted her lips, biting the inside of her cheek. She didn't know whether to be angry, relieved, or scared. "You haven't spoken to him in the last couple of days, have you?"

Marisa's brow furrowed. "No, why?"

Julie, the coward, slunk away.

Sabina pulled in a deep breath and smiled, waving her hands in the air. It was the middle of the party, and there was no need to cause a scene. She knew exactly how Marisa would react. It would break her heart, and she would not try to hide it, no matter who was around. "I'll explain later. Let me take your coat and suitcase into the office. Get yourself something to eat. Julie and Zoey have outdone themselves."

Marisa dutifully surrendered her jacket and suitcase, and Sabina bustled them into the office. With her back to the crowd, propping the case against the desk, Sabina's smile faded and her eyes shifted around the room, trying to calm her nerves. She should have known she would have to be the one to break the news. She just wasn't expecting to be bombarded by it out of nowhere. She thought she could get through the party and then deal with it. But that was life, at least for Sabina, constantly full of sharp, hidden turns—and no way to prepare for it.

CHAPTER 13

*S*abina checked the Movado watch on her left wrist; eight-thirty. The party was already winding down, though for Sabina it felt a bit drawn out with Marisa there, who was the only one not clued in on her big change of circumstance. Patterson, someone she worried might spill the beans, was nowhere to be seen. Maybe he'd grown tired of slumming and left, although his three helpers seemed attached to the wine table, flirting with Robert Martin and giggling. 'Charlie's Angels' indeed.

"Lovely party, Sabina." Mrs. Ellsworth rearranged the mink stole around her sagging neck and allowed her stooped husband to take her arm. The old man steered her toward the door. "I'll be calling you next week to talk about my conservatory," she called over her shoulder.

"I look forward to it. Good night," Sabina replied, giving her a wide smile.

Todd appeared with the last of the figs, trying to entice the remaining guests to try them. But Mrs. Ellsworth's departure seemed to inspire those remaining to make their exit as well. Todd moved to stand behind the table with Julie while Sabina stationed herself by the door, thanking everyone for coming and handing out the last of the brochures.

Finally, only the Patterson entourage remained. One of them glanced at her watch and scowled.

"Is there a problem?" Sabina asked the singular brunette.

One of the other girls blushed, moving forward enough to lower her voice, but not shield her words from the rest of them. "It's Charles. He went to the mens' room and hasn't returned. He has a bit of a problem. Sometimes it takes him a while," she added confidentially.

More information than I needed to know, Sabina thought.

Zoey joined her mother and Todd. "Why don't those vapid chicks go home? My ankles are swollen and I want to sit down."

"So, sit down," Julie hissed. "In fact, why don't you go wait in the truck."

Zoey snatched the chef's hat from her head. "I think I will!" She stalked toward the office where she'd stashed her coat hours before.

"Catfight," Todd whispered.

Julie shook her head. "She had plans for tonight and had to come work with me instead. Thanks for helping, Todd. You're a lifesaver. And by the way, you're great at this. If you're ever looking for supplemental income, I'll hire you on the spot as a server."

He untied the apron around his waist, his chin high with a look of pride. "I very much appreciate the offer, but as of tonight, I'm working for Ms. Reigns."

Sabina joined them, her gaze drifting toward at the bathroom door. She waved her hand at Todd without looking in his direction. "Call me Sabina—and remember, you're only here on a trial basis."

Todd nodded and hurried over to Julie. "Of course. Here, let me fold that table for you, Julie."

The redhead with Patterson glanced at the wall clock, absently tapping her left foot, her annoyance palpable.

What was taking the old goat so long?

Thoughts of food poisoning filled Sabina's head. It would be so like Charles to crash her party, sample the food and drink, then head for the bathroom and swallow ipecac just to be able to say she'd made him sick.

Finally, Sabina mustered her courage and walked toward the door. On the way, she glanced at the vintner who was packing up what was left behind the bar. "I'll go check on him. Robert, would you mind coming with me?"

Robert looked like he did mind since he had to peel the blonde's arm from his own to accompany Sabina, but he did follow her.

Sabina passed through the kitchenette and into the hall. She rapped her knuckles against the bathroom door, leaning toward it. "Charles, are you okay?"

No sound.

She tried the handle. Locked. "Charles?"

Still no answer.

Sabina looked down to see a puddle of water inching its way into the hall. She reached for a flat key that sat atop the molding above the door, then hesitated. "Uh, Robert, would you—I don't want to embarrass the man."

She stepped back, handing Robert the key. He opened the door and poked his head inside, immediately going rigid.

All kinds of horrors ran through Sabina's mind. Did the old man blow up the bathroom? Had he died in there? What was she going to find right after her incredibly successful opening party?

"What's the matter? I swear, if he decided to get one over on me by kicking the bucket in my bathroom, we're moving shop. I don't care how much it costs. I'll be damned if I'm working in a place haunted by him."

Robert backed away, stumbling into Sabina, stepping on her toes.

"Ouch!" Sabina grimaced, lifting her foot.

Robert stuttered slightly. "He's not in there, but—"

The puddle kept growing—the source of the water evident. From the toilet came a rainbow cascade of polyester cords, complete with tassels that hung from the bowl, their white plastic holders discarded in the ever-widening puddle threatening to escape onto the showroom floor.

Sabina pushed Robert aside and made a leap for the shutoff valve under the tank, quickly turning it until the flow stopped.

"Todd!" Sabina called. "We've got a huge problem. Welcome to your first day on the job."

CHAPTER 14

$\mathcal{I}$n all, it was a not so great ending to what had been an auspicious beginning of the evening. While Sabina and Todd cleaned up the mess in the bathroom and hall, she could hear Patterson's associates bickering in the showroom about who was going to pay for their Uber, since their boss had left in a hurry and stranded them.

The bastard.

How petty of him to try—and nearly succeed—to ruin Sabina's grand-opening bash!

Marisa suddenly appeared at the edge of where the puddle had been, arms crossed, looking annoyed. She watched as Sabina mopped up the last of the water. "Mom, what's going on?"

Sabina sighed, shaking her head as she plopped the mop back into the bucket. With his back to Marisa, Steve winked at Sabina as he took the bucket and headed toward the back of the building. Sabina was glad he was there, and that he had enough sense to realize her daughter had no clue what was going on.

"Obviously, the toilet overflowed," she said and headed away from the bathroom.

"Mom," Marisa wailed, stopping Sabina in her tracks. "I heard people snickering and looking at me funny. Something's going on and you need to tell me about it."

Sabina let out a shaky breath. It was the moment she'd dreaded—but what she'd known would be inevitable. "Honey, your Dad's got a surprise for you at home, only it isn't a good one."

Marisa exhaled loudly. "Mother, I'm an adult. I can take any news you have to tell me."

Sabina glanced up at Julie, who'd retreated to the front of the shop, and back over at Marisa. She searched her daughter's face, looking for a sign, a confirmation that when the news was unleashed, she would be okay. She was eighteen. Legally an adult, but with only two months away at college, she was hardly mature.

Marisa pouted. "Mom. Come on!"

Sabina closed her eyes and breathed deeply. "Your father has asked me for a divorce."

Marisa's eyes widened, her mouth dropping open. "What did you do wrong?"

Sabina closed her eyes again briefly. Marisa was daddy's little girl to the end. "I didn't do anything. Honey, your father has," she used his words, "met someone else."

Marisa's brow went up and she put her hands out. "And you're just going to let him leave?"

Sabina let out a breath and saw Julie slinking back farther into the showroom to give them more privacy. "He asked *me* to leave."

"And you didn't fight to keep him?" Before Sabina could explain, Marisa's eyes narrowed in betrayal. "All those e-mails you sent about buying furniture. That was for your new house, wasn't it?"

Sabina wrinkled her nose. "It's not exactly a house."

Marisa crossed her arms over her chest in an almost threatening manner. "So, you've already moved on?"

Sabina held out her hands in supplication. "I didn't have much choice."

"Why didn't you tell me this before now?" Her voice rose. "You lied. In every note you wrote me, you lied."

Sabina held her ground. "No, I didn't. I said as much as I was able to. I told you the truth. Your father agreed to tell you about the situation and he didn't. Apparently, he had many opportunities to do so and chose not to."

Marisa grabbed her coat and purse from the chair. "I'm going home."

She rubbed the fingers of her right hand against her forehead, not looking forward to the car ride. "You'll have to wait until I can lock up and—"

"I'm not going with *you*. I'm going *home*." She stormed out of the office.

Julie stood nearby packing the last of the dishes away.

"Aunt Julie, can you drive me home?"

Julie shot Sabina a look. She gave her a brief nod. Julie sighed and smiled at Marisa. "Sure, kiddo."

Marisa flounced out the door, climbed into the truck, and slammed the door.

"She'll cool off," Julie said.

Sabina gritted her teeth. "Yes, but will I? That stinking rat Jonathan."

Julie shook her head and folded the top in on the carton. "You have at least a week to straighten it all out. I'm heading out. Call if you need me." Julie gave Sabina a hug and she held the door open for Julie as she loaded the last box into the back of the truck. With a wave, she was off.

Todd emerged from the rear of the shop, back in his pinstripes and looking almost regal. "If it's any consolation, the rest of the event went off pretty well."

Sabina's head snapped toward him with a glare. He didn't seem to pick up what had just happened.

"Are we working tomorrow, boss?"

Sabina turned back to where Marisa had stood. "I'm not your boss," she called to Todd over her shoulder.

"But you *will* be," he insisted.

Sabina turned and rolled her eyes. "If you've got nothing better going, then come on in around ten. I'm sure I can find something to keep you busy."

Todd rubbed his hands together excitedly. "Ooh, I like those hours. Will there be leftover champagne and other goodies?"

Sabina just glared at him. "Good night, Todd."

He practically danced out the door. Sabina switched off the lights, found her keys in her purse, and headed for the exit. She locked everything, checking it several times before turning to leave. Most of the other shops in the swanky strip mall were closed, so the parking lot was pretty much empty and still.

As she headed for her lone car, she saw the silhouette of a tall man leaning against the front fender. For a moment she wondered if she should go back to the shop, but then the man straightened and waved. "Sabina, it's me, Steve."

Sabina put her hand to her chest and jogged over. "Are you trying to scare the bejeebers out of me?"

He met her halfway, slung an arm around her shoulders and walked her to her car. "How'd it go with your daughter? I figured it would be best if I bowed out after putting the mop in the back."

"Yeah," Sabina said sadly. "I appreciate that. It didn't go very well."

He turned around, walking backward in front of her, holding her hands. "Can I interest you in a little chana masala, garlic naan, and a bottomless glass of wine?"

All the muscles in her body suddenly went slack and she felt like rolling into a ball at his feet. Instead, she pulled him to a stop and leaned into him. "Oh, I'd love to, Steve. But I have a feeling my evening isn't over. Once Marisa finds out what's waiting for her at home, she's going to be calling me in tears."

Steve placed both hands on her shoulders and leaned in for a kiss. His lips were warm and tender, exactly what Sabina needed. The feeling of him close almost invigorated her, pushing a tiny bit more life into her body. He pulled back. "Rain check?"

She smiled at him and reached around, pulling open the car door. "You bet."

* * *

THE PHONE STARTED RINGING JUST as Sabina opened the door to her lonely little apartment. She hadn't turned up the heat that morning, and the plummeting temperatures made the place feel as cold and damp as her spirits. She groaned as she hurried inside, throwing her bag on the counter and grabbing her cell phone out of her purse.

"Hello?"

"She cleaned out my room!" Marisa wailed, her voice choked with sobs.

Sabina shook her head, knowing she shouldn't be surprised, but still feeling anger rise up in her. "Oh, honey, I'm so sorry. Your dad promised me you'd have a place to come home to. Where's all your stuff?"

"I don't know," Marisa snapped. "There's a crib in here. They painted it yellow—YELLOW!" She screamed, as though this was the ultimate insult.

Sabina winced, knowing full well that Marisa hated that color. What a way to add insult to injury. "Where are you?"

Marisa sniffed. "In your old workroom. That's where they stuck me. There's only a single bed. It's just horr-horr-horrible. Can I come stay with you?"

Sabina looked around. "Oh, Missy, my apartment is only a one-bedroom little hole in the wall."

"*Please*, Mom," Marisa pleaded.

The strain and betrayal in her voice were like a knife thrust into Sabina's heart. "I'll be right there, sweetheart."

Ten minutes later, Sabina was ringing the doorbell on what used to be her home. Every muscle in her body was coiled to attack, and like a lioness, she sprang as soon as Jonathan answered.

Sabina jammed her finger into Jonathan's chest. "Listen to me, you sonofabitch, you promised you'd tell Marisa about you and your little paramour. Now look at the mess you've made."

"I meant to tell her," he grumbled. "It just seemed easier to wait."

"Oh please," Sabina groaned. "Just admit it, you were too much of a chicken shit to actually go through with what you said. What is it with men like you? You act like a doting father and then suddenly, when you have some sort of mid-life crisis, you unlearn everything about being a decent parent *and* human being. And why did you have to clear out *her* room for the nursery?"

"Courtney wanted—"

Sabina put up her hand and cut him off. "Marisa was in your life for eighteen years before Courtney appeared. You're just as much her father as you are to this new baby, and you'd *better* live up to your responsibilities."

Jonathan threw back his shoulders, his expression growing cold. "Technically, I don't have any responsibilities. Marisa is eighteen and—"

Who the hell was this man standing before her? He wasn't the Jonathan she'd known, loved and shared a child with. He was some kind of Courtney worker-bee come to life, ready to serve the new Queen's every whim.

Sabina had heard enough and brushed past him. "Marisa. It's Mom. Let's go."

A door slammed and Marisa appeared at the top of the stairs. Dragging her suitcase behind her, she took them two at a time, and shoved past Jonathan, bursting out into the darkness.

Sabina glared at Jonathan, not daring to raise her voice above a whisper. "You'll be hearing from my lawyer."

She grabbed the door's brass handle and slammed it shut behind her.

Marisa had sniffled on the ride over, staring out the side window and declining to speak. Sabina let her wallow in her grief. She'd come home in what she'd thought would be joy, only to see her whole world turned upside down and destroyed. Only time could heal that kind of wound.

Sabina had hoped the phone would be ringing by the time they arrived at her apartment, with Jonathan calling to apologize and begging Missy to come home. But it sat sullenly on the end table, refusing to make a peep.

Walking inside, Marisa shrugged out of her coat and laid it on a chair, looking around Sabina's sterile little apartment, disdain shimmering off of her in waves. The waterworks started again as tears overflowed her eyes. "What a terrible place."

"Oh, come on," Sabina said, snagging her coat and hanging it in the small hall closet. "It's not as small as your dorm room."

Marisa sneered. "Yes, but we have a common area that's three times bigger than *this*."

Sabina lifted an eyebrow. "And you share it with seven other girls."

Marisa glanced around the place. "Yeah, but there's stuff on the walls and it at least feels homey."

Sabina took in the boring beige walls. "I hadn't planned on staying here long and I've been more interested in getting the shop up to speed. It's the place I feel most at home these days."

Marisa sighed heavily, shaking her head. "I just can't believe that after all these years, Dad has some brain fart or something, tells you he wants a divorce, and you just walk out of the house like it's no big deal."

Sabina stared at her daughter for a long moment not wanting to fight, but already tired of being blamed. "I know you're eighteen and you haven't had a serious relationship, but you're more than capable of seeing this for what it is. Your father wasn't working late all those nights last summer; he was seeing your soon-to-be stepmother the whole time."

"Don't call her that," Marisa snarled. "She's not any kind of mother to me."

Sabina sighed and collapsed onto one of the bar stools at the kitchen's peninsula. "I know it's a lot to take in right now, but you can't just sit here and blame me for everything. Over the years, your father and I grew apart. It happens. And sometime early next year, that woman is going to give birth to your brother or sister."

"Half," Marisa pointed out before lowering her shoulders. "But yes, I guess you're right. It still sucks. It's utter bullshit. And now I'm thrown out." She looked around the tiny apartment. "There are homeless box shelters bigger than *this* place. Awesome. Both of my parents kicked me out."

Sabina rolled her eyes. "No one kicked you out. You're here aren't you? And there's still a room at the other house for you—if you'll accept it. Look, your father and I both love you—"

Marisa shook her head, putting her hand up. "Stop. Don't give me that made-for-TV bull crap about how you both love me and that will never change."

With that she stormed off, teetering back and forth before heading into Sabina's bedroom and slamming the door shut. Marisa's reaction hadn't been quite as bad as Sabina thought it would be, but it was definitely bad. Sabina just hoped the situation would improve by the next day.

Of course, by the time the sun rose, Sabina could tell it wasn't even close to being okay or even remotely better. Marisa was at loose ends that morning, but she seemed more restless than upset, and her weepy interludes had grown farther and farther apart. Sabina hadn't mourned the loss of her home as much as Marisa did. Her anxiety had come from jumping into the business world with no real training and the tremendous fear of failure.

"Why don't you come to the shop with me," Sabina said. "At least we have more room to move around there."

Marisa glared at her, shaking her head with a pout. "No, thanks." Then she seemed to think better of it. "Well, maybe. I don't know."

After changing her mind three times, Marisa finally agreed to accompany Sabina to the studio and help in the shop for the day. After all, none of her friends were around yet and she figured she might as well kill time with her mom.

Sabina fought the urge to smack her daughter and won. Another triumph for motherhood.

Todd was waiting in a Prius near the store and sprang from the car with the enthusiasm of a child on Christmas day. Dressed in casual clothes, he looked ready to wait on customers.

Except for the party, Sabin hadn't sent out a press release to let the world at large know her shop was open, and the company she had contracted to put vinyl lettering on the door giving the hours of operation hadn't yet made an appearance. That was fine. There was still so much to do. The storeroom was filled with boxes that needed to be emptied and the merchandise put out for display. They had their work cut out for them, but Sabina was also prepared to wait on any customers who were brave enough to come through the doors.

Marisa had never had a job before, but she seemed to like unpacking and admiring the baubles. Sabina showed her a few basics of display and left her and Todd to do the task while she worked in the office.

The first item on her agenda was a call to Jonathan. Marisa wanted the belongings she'd left behind and Sabina needed to know when it would be convenient to pick them up. The last thing she really wanted was to have to call him. Just the sound of his breathing made her cringe these days.

Sabina dialed her former phone number.

"Hello?" Courtney answered.

"I'd like to speak to Jonathan," Sabina said, keeping her tone even despite the urge to let loose on the woman.

"Whom may I say is calling?" She knew very well who was calling.

"His *wife*." After all, according to the law, she still was.

A long silence followed, then she heard the sound of the phone being put down. It took a minute or more before Jonathan picked up. "Sabina?"

There were no frills to the conversation. "Marisa wants her things. When can we get them?"

She could visualize Jonathan checking his watch. "I'll be free this afternoon."

Sabina glanced at her calendar. It wasn't at all full, but if she was going to go over to her former home, she wanted to make it difficult for Jonathan. Anything to make his life a little bit harder was fine with her. "Well, I'm not. I have a business to run and Saturday is possibly my busiest day of the week. How about tomorrow morning before ten?"

He exhaled into the phone—a snort of impatience. "That's quite inconvenient."

"For whom? All we're asking is for a ten- to fifteen-minute window." Sabina bristled at his arrogance.

"Yes, but you don't understand—"

Sabina cut him off. "Don't understand what? That your paramour can't accept the fact that you already *have* a child—a child who is bewildered that her entire life has been turned upside down. That you turned her room into a nursery for a child who will take her place in your life."

Jonathan was calm, almost as though he knew what was coming before Sabina said it.

"I never said that."

"Yes, well that's the way Missy interpreted it."

"You have no idea where I'm coming from," Jonathan said defensively.

Sabina laughed wildly. "And I don't give a damn. You're Marisa's father. Dammit all, act like it!"

Jonathan huffed. "You think this is so simple for me. I have a loyalty to Courtney now, but I still love Marisa very much. That said, Marisa is a *very* negative person, and she gets it from *you*. Courtney did nothing wrong in moving her room to your old craft space. Marisa will only be home every now and then, and the baby will be here every day."

"Well, Courtney can have fun with the craft room now, because the whole damn place is hers. We'll be there at nine-thirty. Have her stuff ready." Sabina said and slammed down the phone.

Sabina growled in frustration. She was glad Marisa was eighteen. She wasn't sure how she would have navigated co-parenting with her soon-to-be-ex if she weren't. Sabina would have probably just suffocated him in his own ego and been done with it. Regardless, the time was set and all she had to do was get Marisa's stuff and haul it back to her apartment and then figure out how to store it.

Todd stuck his head around the corner. "Hey, do we put out all the cabinet knobs or just one of each for display?"

Sabina narrowed her eyes, speaking in an overly happy tone. "Todd. Just the kind of employee I was looking for. What are you doing tomorrow?"

Todd's expression darkened. "Whatever it is, I'm now assuming it won't be something that I'll be chomping at the bit to do."

Sabina grinned. "Good, now all I need is some kind of a moving truck to snatch Marisa's stuff."

"Oh," Todd said, pulling out his phone. "I got this. I have friends everywhere. I'll take care of it."

Sabina folded her hands in front of her. "Perfect."

CHAPTER 15

*A*t precisely nine o'clock, Sabina answered the knock at her apartment door. Dressed in jeans, a plain purple sweatshirt and sneakers, she was ready to tote barges and lift bales...or at least the flotsam and jetsam of Marisa's life-long accumulation of stuff. Todd arrived right on time with a cardboard tray with three cups of Starbucks coffee.

"Are you ladies ready? I've got the truck and even brought refreshments." He proffered a white bakery bag and offered up the coffee.

"You shouldn't have done that," Sabina said but grabbed a cup, nonetheless.

Todd's eyes practically twinkled. "I've gotta keep the wheels greased if you're going to hire me."

Sabina didn't even bother to refute him. What was the point? She had a feeling she would be doing anything she could to make room for him by the end of all of it. After all, he was going beyond the duties of an assistant by helping her move Marisa's things. "Let me get my coat. I can eat on the way."

"Where's Marisa?" Todd asked.

Sabina shrugged on her coat. "She isn't coming."

"It would be too mortifying," came a muffled voice from the bedroom. Marisa slouched into the living room. Even in mismatched sweats with her hair in an untidy ponytail, she looked terrific. She grabbed her coffee with a muttered, "Thanks," and taking a gulp before flopping down into the chintz armchair.

Todd gave her a reassuring smile. "I don't blame you, kiddo. I'm sure your mom and I can handle it all."

Sabina scoffed angrily as she grabbed her purse. "You shouldn't have to handle any of it. Jonathan should pack the truck himself. He should *pay* for the truck. You didn't have to pay for the truck did you, Todd?"

Todd waved his hands and shook his head. "I told you. I have friends in the trade. I have friends in *every* trade."

Todd's plan to worm his way into Sabina's affections was working far too well. And he always seemed to have the tools or the knowledge she needed at any given moment. Either it was kismet or the guy knew exactly what he was doing. Either way, Sabina was not about to complain.

She leaned over and kissed her daughter on the forehead, ignoring her sneer. "I'll call you before we leave the house, Missy."

"I'll be right here. After all, I've got nowhere else to go." Marisa hung her head and sighed like a death-row prisoner.

It took everything Sabina had not to roll her eyes and groan. Todd sipped his coffee and headed for the door. "Later, kiddo."

"And don't call me kiddo," Marisa growled as the door closed behind them.

* * *

JONATHAN'S MERCEDES was parked in the driveway—not his usual style. It looked bereft in the gray morning light. The swollen clouds overhead appeared ready to gush at any moment. Sabina scoped out the home's grounds as though on a black ops mission. There was no sign of Courtney's car anywhere. It was probably parked in the garage—safe and protected from the elements.

God, I hate the woman who took my place.

It was a useless sentiment, she knew, but it was wavering at the surface of her emotions every time she had to come back to this place she used to call home. It was weird, having another person just move in and pick up where she left off. She wondered if it was weird for Courtney. Probably, which was why she'd rearranged everything, painted everything, and changed the place as much as she could without completely knocking it down and starting over. Sabina almost wished she would have.

Todd and Sabina exited the truck. Sabina felt a twinge of gratitude in her chest, happy to have Todd there with her. It wasn't like she expected a fight like in an action flick or anything, but just not being there by herself made the whole thing a little less intimidating. She didn't want to go there alone. Hell, she didn't want to go there at all!

Todd paused at the truck's back door. "I'll open up and get the dolly."

Sabina nodded and strode toward the house. A raindrop hit her cheek as she approached the steps. It felt odd knocking at her own front door. She'd been so angry two nights before that she hadn't really thought about it until she arrived. She'd repainted that door herself only a week or so before Jonathan's announcement. Bright crimson would be cheerful for the holidays she'd thought. Now Courtney would be feeling cheerful in Sabina's beautiful home. Meanwhile, Sabina would be held hostage in her crummy little apartment. There was nowhere to even put up a decent-sized tree for Christmas. And with Marisa's junk cluttering up the place it would be even more difficult.

Sabina knocked again, glancing down at her watch.

The thumping sound of footsteps preceded the door's opening. She eyed Jonathan, dressed in one of his best sweaters, Dockers, and polished shoes. His expression was neutral. Despite it being Sunday, he looked like he was getting ready to go out to brunch, not jump into a 'kick-your-daughter-out-of-her-own-house' party.

"You're wearing *that* to load a truck?" Sabina asked.

He scowled. "You used to at least observe the routine niceties and say hello."

Sabina rolled her eyes, looking around him. "I'm not here to charm you. I'm here to collect our daughter's things. Remember, you tossed her out of her home. The place you said she'd always be welcome."

His mouth tightened. "She *chose* to leave."

Her lips flattened. "You and Courtney didn't give her much of a choice."

"Marisa could've acted like an adult—"

"She's eighteen years old!" Sabina stopped herself, holding up a hand to keep him from replying. "I don't want to hear any more. I'm not here to argue with you or even hold a conversation longer than it takes to retrieve our daughter's things. Then, don't worry, I'll be out of your hair so you can continue your remodeling."

She made a forward step to push him aside, but he wouldn't let her enter the former home that held only a slight eerie resemblance to what it had once been. "Her things are in the garage."

Sabina's stomach tightened. "Then open the door and let's get this over with."

She turned her back on him and bounced forward with her chin high, joining Todd at the truck. The front door closed with a jolt a that made Sabina jump. Todd watched Jonathan as he crossed the patch of lawn and headed for the garage. "Not real warm and welcoming, is he?"

Sabina scoffed. "You have no idea. He's in what I like to call 'lawyer mode' right now," she said, making air quotes with her fingers. "He isn't showing any emotion toward anyone. I can tell he's nervous though, he keeps scratching his right thigh."

Todd narrowed his eyes and watched. Sure enough, as Jonathan fumbled around looking for something in his, left pocket, he stopped and scratched his right leg. Todd smirked. "That has to be weird, knowing someone so well you can call their little weird ticks."

Sabina frowned. "It used to be endearing, a true sign of the depth of our relationship. Now, it's an annoying waste of three seconds of my life."

Jonathan finally took the keys from his pocket and unlocked the garage's side door, reaching inside to press the button for the garage door opener. The door obligingly rose to reveal twenty or thirty large black plastic trash bags strewn across the dusty concrete floor.

Sabina's blood pressure rose at least a hundred points. She glared at Jonathan, stomping forward. "You tossed Marisa's possessions into plastic bags like they were trash?"

Jonathan groaned as though he expected it. "Where was I supposed to get boxes at the last minute?"

Sabina's brows both rose and she snarled. "U-Haul. Any liquor or grocery store, the back of a convenience store. Hell, you can go on social media and people are *giving* away moving boxes away for free all the time."

Jonathan sniffed. "I don't slum for used boxes."

"And you don't respect your daughter enough to show some care for the things she holds dear, either." Sabina stared down at the lumpy bags. Clothes, mostly, she figured. What about the bed and the other furniture?

Sabina glanced up at Jonathan. "This is it?"

Jonathan frowned and looked away.

She shook her head and leaned in front of him so he could see her. "Where's her bed?"

He kept his nose in the air, knowing full well he was wrong, but standing behind it anyway. "We need it as a guest bed. Courtney's invited some of her family for the holiday weekend."

Sabina's anger quotient rose another ten points. "And where was Marisa supposed to sleep in the meantime?"

Jonathan shrugged. "I assume the same place she slept last night."

On the couch—every time she visits? Sabina took a deep breath and thought about it. Why was she worried? Her apartment was too small to accommodate her daughter's bedroom furniture anyway. She'd obviously have to speed up her search for a more permanent living arrangement. But first, she needed to get this whole situation under control. She couldn't believe she had to ask her daughter's own father where she was supposed to sleep. It was infuriating.

Sabina searched Jonathan's face, studying the newly formed lines around his eyes. "Why are you doing this? Why are being so cold toward Marisa?"

"You're exaggerating again," Jonathan scoffed, blowing her off. "Besides, she's not a child anymore."

Sabina crossed her arms. "And you don't seem to be a father, either."

Jonathan's head snapped toward Sabina's. "This isn't easy on me either, you know."

Sabina pursed her lips, leaning back on her heels. "Pardon me if I can't muster any sympathy for you."

As they talked, Todd took control and started to load bags into the back of the moving truck. Sabina was thankful once again for having him there with her. There was no telling how long she would have stood there blabbering and fighting with the big dumb idiot in front of her without a distraction.

Sabina swiped her hands through the air, closing her eyes. "Look, let's just get this done. The sooner these bags are in that truck, the sooner you can get me—and your daughter—out of your hair."

Jonathan shook his head, snatching a bag from the ground and walking it toward the truck. Sabina leaned down and picked up two of them, glancing up at Todd. He gave her a small smirk and winked as he picked another up and slung it over his shoulder like Santa Claus. With the three of them moving the bags, everything was packed and loaded into the truck within five minutes. Of course, it wasn't as though it was any great mystery on how to fit Marisa's things in the back, they were slung in there like the local trash man had come by on his weekly route.

It was what it was though, and it would serve no purpose for Sabina to get all up in arms over every little detail. She knew that somewhere, deep down in the hollow shell of the man that Jonathan had become, there was still a small tendril of his old self. And that old self was ridden with guilt. Guilt over their marriage, guilt over his cheating, and guilt over how he was treating his first-born child. One day it would come back to bite him in the ass, and Sabina thought she would relish that day. Until then, she had to continue focusing on her own life and on Marisa's well being. If Jonathan wasn't going to be a parent to Marisa anymore, she would just have to pick up the slack.

After Jonathan had thrown the last bag in the truck, he turned and walked away, hitting the button to the garage door. Sabina didn't even give him another second's notice, helping Todd close the back of the truck and jumping in the cab's passenger seat. She knew Jonathan stopped to awkwardly say something in retreat, but it felt good to know he was met with her backside. She glanced in the mirror as they pulled away, finding him standing in the yard, randomly looking around as though he was lost. She couldn't even remember what she had ever seen in him.

"That was productive, and maybe therapeutic even," Todd said with a shrug.

Sabina shook her head and gave a mirthless laugh. "I swear he wasn't some heartless zombie when I was married to him. At least not for the first fifteen years of the twenty we survived."

"If I may offer an opinion," Todd said as they drove down the road.

"Go ahead."

"It seems to me that your soon-to-be-ex has found himself in a situation that he has no idea how to get himself out of. And because of that, he's wandering around like a blithering idiot. It just goes to show you that men blast full speed ahead when they think the situation is fun but have absolutely no clue what consequences they'll have to face later on."

Sabina turned to look at him. "All men?"

"Just the clueless kind," he replied.

"Yeah, well Jonathan can face all those consequences on his own because I no longer have a responsibility to help and support him. If Courtney wants marriage and babies, she can do the dirty work, too, from now on."

Sabina couldn't help but smile to herself, picturing perfect, petite Courtney, pregnant, and dressed to the nines, unable to understand why Jonathan wasn't that suave and debonair man he was when they were sneaking around behind her back. Eventually, she would realize he wasn't in it for her, he was in it for the excitement and the thrill. Sabina was sure Jonathan would soon feel his little side action was a lot more interesting when she was off-limits.

CHAPTER 16

*M*arisa was gone when Todd and Sabina arrived back at the apartment. A Post-It note on the fridge said she'd been 'rescued by friends. Will call later.'

Teenagers.

"I guess we're responsible for making sure her things get inside as well," Sabina sighed, shaking her head. "If it weren't for the fact that her father just abandoned her, I would make her come back or leave her bags out in front of the door."

Todd shook his head and grinned, stretching his shoulders. "It's all right. We'll get it done. Besides, maybe time with her friends will take that constant dragging expression off of her pretty face."

Sabina lifted a brow. "No, that's permanently displayed. It's been there since the moment she turned fifteen. It was gradual before that, but definitely became a scowl at fifteen."

Todd waved an arm back toward the door. "Come on, keep going or you'll lose your momentum."

Sabina tossed her bag on the counter and shuffled across the room toward the door. "My momentum left about ten years ago. I've been continuing to move solely based on the amount of caffeine consumed, and the importance of the event I was heading to. This would rank at about a two on my scale of importance."

Todd smiled at Sabina. "But a ten on Marisa's which is why you're still moving."

She shrugged and, with a deep sigh, moved along behind him as he opened the back of the truck and started passing her the bags. They dragged everything into Sabina's tiny living room. By the time they'd retrieved the last one, the room looked even smaller. The work she'd done to create a look of country chic now looked more like a close replica of the county dump, minus the stench.

Tossing the last bag on the pile, Sabina collapsed onto one of the stools at the peninsula and raised a hand in benediction. "You are now free for the rest of the day. You are hereby released from the chains that bind you."

Todd shook his head with a laugh. "Oh, no. I'm not leaving it like this. Now we go to Walmart and buy a ton of totes. You've got to store all this stuff one way or another, even if you go out next week and buy your dream home. Totes will keep it all tidy and accessible. I love those things. You can even put them in Self-Storage and they stay sealed, dry, and free from vermin and weather. Besides, look at it this way, if she comes home to a mess, her attitude will follow and *you* will have to deal with that. If she comes home and can easily find everything, has all of her things, and there's no stress, she may actually sigh at you half as many times as usual."

Sabina squinted up at him. "Do you always think of everything?"

Todd straightened proudly. "I'm very efficient. And by the end of the week, you'll find that you can't function without me."

He reached down to help Sabina up. She groaned, letting her head fall back as he pulled her to her feet. She only made it two steps before her cell phone started ringing. Her heart skipped a beat thinking it was Marisa with some sort of problem. It was the same feeling she had once her daughter started going out without parental supervision. It was just automatic. It wasn't like Marisa did anything to combat that, and the girl was reckless when she was upset. At that moment, on a scale of one to ten, Marisa's dramatic emotional state was about a twenty.

When Sabina looked down at the screen, her heart flipped again, but in a different, more pleasant way. It was Steve. "Hello."

"Hey there," Steve said, his voice more welcoming than Sabina had expected. "How about that rain check tonight?"

Sabina's mouth drooped into a frown. "Oh, Steve, I'd love to, but my daughter Marisa is here and—"

Todd waved his arms, nearly jumping out of his skin in excitement.

"Hang on, will you?" Sabina put her hand over the receiver. "What's wrong? Did you see a spider?"

Todd let his arms fall shaking his head. "Go out with—what's his name? Steve? Trust me, Marisa is going to want to wash every article of clothing, iron them, and organize according to color, style, and size. She will be occupied for hours and hours."

Sabina's mouth dropped open. "My never-lift-a-finger daughter? Boy, you have impeccable abilities to organize, but you are not very good at reading people."

Todd pursed his lips. "You don't know the power of a teenager's scorn. She is right now, casting magical, mystical voodoo spells on her father's new woman. She's wishing that she could march right over there and snatch the proverbial wig right off her head. But she can't so she'll be hell-bent on erasing anything that could remind her that the woman exists. She'll want to swab down every knick-knack, book, and cosmetic to excise any cooties Courtney may have deposited on them. I'll keep her company. Maybe show her how to properly store an ironed blouse. Besides, I'm good at keeping people busy so they don't even realize that it's happening."

Sabina shook her head. "I can't ask you to babysit—"

Todd smacked his hands together loudly, pursing his lips with his hand on his hip. "Do you want a shot with this guy or not?"

She did.

Taking her hand off the mouthpiece, she summoned some cheer into her voice. "What time?"

* * *

ONCE MARISA REAPPEARED AN HOUR LATER, she hung her head, tears welling in her eyes at the sight of all the trash bags littering the living room floor. But as Todd predicted, she did indeed intend to sanitize every item she owned that had come in contact with 'that evil bitch,' as she had officially christened Courtney. She didn't even seem to care that Sabina had a date.

Come to think of it, Sabina hadn't considered that dinner with Steve actually constituted a date until she started searching her closet and realized she wasn't satisfied with a single thing inside of it.

Todd appeared in her bedroom doorway and tilted his head at her. "Why do you look lost? This place is tiny."

Sabina pinched the bridge of her nose, not wanting to admit it, but knowing she needed some help. "I haven't been out with a man, besides Jonathan, in a very long time. At least not a planned," she hesitated, "outing."

"Date," Todd interjected, looking at Sabina with no change of expression.

She cleared her throat nervously. "Date," she reluctantly admitted. "I don't have anything to wear."

Todd pushed up his sleeves, marched dramatically over to the closet, and skimmed through her clothes. He tsked-tsked Sabina and gave her a glance before pulling out a fitted pink sweater and black palazzo pants. He held them up to her, clutching his chin with his hand as though he were Alexander Wang dressing her for his next big show. After a few moments, Todd nodded. "You'll look gorgeous. Put these on, do a little fluff with your hair and shazam, the new and ready-to-date Sabina will appear. Now, where do you keep the Woolite? Marisa and I have *real* work to do."

Hours later, when the doorbell rang, there was a mad dash to open it. Marisa got there first of course, slightly thrown off by two men standing on the other side. One was the pizza delivery guy and the other was Steve. Marisa glanced over at Sabina, who was adjusting her earring. "Do you need money for the pizza?"

Marisa shook her head, pulling a wad of cash from her back pocket. "My treat."

Sabina could almost see the judgment in Marisa's eyes as she handed the delivery guy a tip, staring at Steve's heavy Carhartt jacket and work boots. He was dressed nicely in jeans and a button-up shirt, but definitely a different look than her father. Sabina stepped back, glancing over at the perfectly primed-and-pressed Todd and back at Steve before clearing her throat and moving out of the way.

Sabina pecked Marisa on the forehead as she passed, waving at Todd. "Goodnight. If you need anything, you know how to get a hold of me."

"Have fun, love birds," Todd said and giggled.

Marisa furrowed her brow and elbowed Todd who quickly wiped the smile off his face. Sabina shook her head and smiled, closing the door behind her. When she turned, she stumbled a bit, finding herself almost nose to nose with Steve. He grinned and held her elbow, steadying her. They stared at each other for a few awkward moments before Steve shrugged deeper into his jacket, his smile wry. "Is Indian okay with you?"

"It sounds fantastic," Sabina replied, gathering herself. "You've been promising me for weeks."

He laughed as they turned, reaching for Sabina's hand and holding it tightly as they headed down the walk toward his truck.

His hand was cold thanks to the November temperatures, but the warmth in Sabina's chest made up for it. For the first time in days, her shoulders relaxed, the tension in her face eased, and her heart fluttered happily. If this was to be her new normal, she had a feeling she could get used to it really fast. Happy looked good on her, and she was starting to think that life was finally starting to smooth out.

* * *

THE RESTAURANT WAS MORE crowded than Sabina would have predicted. Calm pink wallpaper with velvety hues of greens, and culturally themed art decorated the otherwise plain room. Crisp white linens donned each table, and quiet, eerily strange music came from hidden speakers. Nothing ostentatious, just simple and elegant.

Sabina and Jonathan surrendered their jackets to the entryway rack and stepped up to the register. Unfamiliar spices scented the warm air.

"Your usual table, Steve?" the tall waiter asked.

Steve nodded with a smile. "Naturally."

Approaching the linen-covered table, Steve pulled out Sabina's chair. She put her clutch under her arm and smiled at him as she sat. He walked around the table and took a seat across from her. Sabina happily poked at the bright crimson napkins folded pyramid style in front of her. The waiter, dressed in black pants, a white shirt, and a knee-length black apron leaned carefully over and filled their glasses with water.

Steve smiled at the server and waited for him to walk away before opening the menu. Sabina glanced at the hundred different choices, nothing sounding familiar to her. She didn't want to seem as though she had never tried anything new, but her choices were to ask his opinion or end up with something she may or may not enjoy. To avoid accidentally ordering a flaming entree, she decided to play it safe. "What do you recommend?"

Steve closed his menu and nodded to the center of the room. "A lot of people are turned off by hot curries, especially if they've never had this type of food before. I think you should play it safe and just sample the buffet. It's mostly vegetarian, but you won't believe the flavors. Later, when you're acclimated, I'll introduce you to some of the hotter dishes."

Oh, that sounded like he intended to hang around a while. Sabina didn't mind in the least, she had no curfew, really no one to answer to. She was free to make her own choices, even if she had to continue to remind herself she wasn't doing anything wrong. Twenty years in a relationship ground some things into a person's brain that took an effort to remove. It was worth it though, and every time Sabina reminded herself that she was free, a whisper of thrill and excitement flooded through her.

"What are you doing for Thanksgiving?" Sabina asked, putting down the menu.

Steve laid his menu on top of hers, both of them waiting for the waiter to come back. "My son, David, is supposed to come home for the holiday. I haven't seen him since he left for school in September."

Sabina tried not to act thrown off. She hadn't even considered that Steve might have a son, especially not one around the same age as her own daughter. "Where does he go?"

Steve beamed. "Colorado State. It's a good school, but I think he wanted to go there as an excuse to get in more snowboarding. He knew he wasn't going to get that much around here."

"He can have the snow," Sabina said.

At that moment the waiter walked back up, nodding to them both. Steve glanced at Sabina and took the lead. "I think we'll both do the buffet this evening."

The waiter nodded. "Very good. You can help yourself whenever you're ready."

LORRAINE BARTLETT

Steve stood up and put out his hand, helping Sabina from her chair. They walked over to the buffet and grabbed plates. Sabina walked along, listening to Steve explain each of the dishes to her, taking a little dab here and a little dab there of the different suggestions he made for her. In all truth, she wasn't really paying that much attention, her eyes too focused on the way his jaw moved when he talked. His cologne was intoxicating and he moved along beside her, leaning down to whisper so they weren't disrupting any of the other patrons.

When they were done, they headed back to the table. Sabina put her napkin in her lap and picked up her fork, taking a bite. The flavors hit her almost instantly, and she nodded with wide eyes. Steve grinned. "Good, huh?"

"Mmm," Sabina replied, taking another bite of rice and dahl—savoring it. "I could get used to this kind of food."

Steve leaned forward. "Why do you think I have a regular table here?"

They both laughed, eating for a few moments in happy silence. Sabina sipped her water and let her eyes rove over Steve for a moment, taking the man in. She was used to his rough demeanor, his clothing covered in dust, but sitting across a dinner table from her was a completely different version of the man. He sported the same smile, the same rugged, handsome vibe, but put together, tidy, and very mannerly.

"Well, it sounds like you'll have a really nice Thanksgiving," Sabina said, trying to keep herself from staring too long.

"How about you?" Steve asked.

Sabina shrugged, accidentally letting out a sigh that sounded far too close to disappointment then she would have wanted. "I hadn't planned anything, figuring Marisa would join Jonathan and Courtney. It doesn't look as though that's going to happen now, so, I don't know. I suppose I'll roast some kind of fowl if that's what Missy wants. I'd just as soon leave the cooking to someone else, though. My apartment is extremely small and I'm not really set up for significant culinary creations. And I'm not sure I know how to cook a feast for only two people."

Steve shook his head. "I can understand that. Well, you're both more than welcome to join us. It's not going to be anything fancy."

Sabina smiled but didn't answer. It was kind of an awkward moment. She licked her lips and looked down at her plate. On one hand, it was incredibly sweet of him to offer, and he had said it without much thought, which meant he didn't have any reservations, but Sabina did. She really liked Steve, but she didn't want to horn in on his time with his son. On top of that, she wasn't quite sure what the rules of engagement stated when a new beau invited you to Thanksgiving so soon after the first date.

All the things Sabina hated about dating came rushing back to her. It was a fifty-fifty shot when you faced those kinds of decisions. She didn't want to be rude and make him think she wasn't interested. But she also didn't want to come off as smothering or too anxious to jump right in. She wasn't even sure if that was a romantic gesture or if it was a mannerly one. She really hated the whole dating world, and it was even more confusing since she hadn't done it for over twenty years.

Sensing her hesitation, Steve changed the subject. "Do you watch football?"

Sabina looked up at him with a smile, and relief. "Um, not really. I used to, but in years past it became a thing where Jonathan watched football with his guy friends and the rest of us woman folk were forced to drink wine in the kitchen."

Steve laughed. "I'll be honest; with the way the sport has changed over the years you might have gotten the better deal."

Sabina smiled, glancing down into her lap as her phone vibrated inside of her purse. She put her hand on top of it and pressed through the fabric, sending it to voicemail. She opened her mouth to respond but the phone vibrated again. She put her fork down and gave Steve a nervous smile. "Sorry. If you could give me one second."

She pulled the phone from her bag and rolled her eyes. "It's just Marisa. She probably wants me to stop on my way back and bring something to her. My money is on ice cream."

Sabina tapped the call icon and put the phone to her ear, smiling at Steve. "Yes, my dear. What is so urgent that you had to—"

"Mom?" The fear in Marisa's voice constricted Sabina's chest.

Sabina sat forward, her smile fading, her fingers digging into the ledge of the table. "What's wrong?"

Marisa's voice trembled. "Courtney called."

Courtney instead of 'that evil bitch.' That couldn't be good. "What did she want?"

Marisa's voice cracked and Sabina could tell she was doing her best to hold back tears. "Dad's in the hospital. They think he had a stroke."

CHAPTER 17

*S*teve stopped the car outside the hospital's emergency entrance, reaching across the shifter and touching Sabina's hand. "I'll meet you inside."

She looked at Steve with surprise. "You don't have to stay, Steve."

He shook his head. "I'll stay until Marisa gets here. I don't want you to be alone."

Sabina nodded, wishing she could bury her face into his shoulder, but it was too soon in their... well, whatever it was they had. Too soon to be that familiar. Instead, she managed a weak smile and climbed out of the truck. Todd was driving Marisa over to meet her, but the restaurant had been closer to the hospital so she got there first.

Sabina walked up to the emergency room's reception desk and gave a concerned smile. "Hello, I just received a call that my, my husband was brought in for a possible stroke? His name is Jonathan Mill—"

"Oh good, you're here," the receptionist nurse said. "If I could have your ID and insurance information for him that would be fantastic. It's been a bit of a debacle. The woman—" She looked at Sabina with a pause, not knowing if it would come as a shock.

"Courtney," Sabina said, reassuring her. "Jonathan is my soon to be ex-husband."

The nurse nodded in understanding. "Well, the young woman is too distraught to be of any assistance."

Chalk one up to maturity.

"Where is she?"

The nurse shrugged. "Maybe getting coffee. She isn't allowed in the treatment area without authorization."

Sabina sighed. "If she comes back to the reception desk, she has my blessing to visit."

"Okay."

The nurse typed the information into the computer, made copies of Sabina's ID and verified Jonathan's insurance, and handed the cards back to her along with a visitors' badge. "This will get you back into the ER with no problem. Just go right to the door to your right and I'll bring you through."

Sabina nodded, glancing back at the ER doors, but Steve wasn't back from parking and Marisa wasn't there yet. She took a deep breath as she stood in front of the frosted window on the automatic doors that separated the waiting room from the ER. Sabina followed the nurse through the maze of hallways in the back until they turned a corner and came to a halt. "I'll let the resident know you're here," the nurse said.

"Thanks." Sabina walked past her, reaching up and pulling the curtain aside just enough to slip through. She straightened it back behind her and turned. Jonathan lay motionless in the emergency room bed, his eyes closed, face pale, and the right side of his mouth drooping slightly downward. An oxygen tube trailed from his nose and wires snaked to an array of machinery that beeped and hummed ominously. The blankets were tucked perfectly around him, and she could tell he hadn't moved a muscle. Her eyes shifted uncomfortably from side to side as she stepped to his side.

She should've felt something, some twinge of sadness or worry, but pity was about all she could muster. The events of the past few months had killed her love for this man. Any residual affection she might've felt had been obliterated by the callous way he'd treated their daughter over the past few days. But as the mother of his child, she could at least wish him well. Marisa would ultimately forgive him.

Sabina wasn't as naïve. If Jonathan pulled through, he would never again be the monster in Marisa's eyes. The only thing Sabina found solace in was that Marisa's anger would be directed straight at Courtney and not her. It would be the first time someone else felt the brunt of Marisa's misplaced anger.

"You sonofabitch," she muttered. "Look what your new life has delivered."

She frowned, feeling just a little guilty, then added, "Isn't Karma a bitch?"

Suddenly the curtain was thrown back and Courtney stood in the opening, a dark Polartec coat hung from her left arm, and the roundness of her belly was evident through her form-fitting pink blouse. Sabina couldn't stop herself from wondering why pregnant women refused to wear maternity clothes. Courtney looked like a snake who'd just swallowed a rat.

Courtney said nothing for a long moment. "Uh...thank you for letting me see him. They wouldn't let me—"

"Rules are rules," Sabina said evenly and shrugged.

"They said I'm not 'family' so they wouldn't tell me anything," she said, her voice breaking.

All sorts of thoughts crowded Sabina's mind. She wasn't sure how to gauge this woman who was not much older than her own child. Was she supposed to comfort her? Sabina wasn't even sure if she wanted to converse with the interloper who'd taken her husband, ostracized her daughter, and was now living in her home—sleeping in her bed—any longer than necessary.

Sabina took in a long deep breath and remembered that she was the adult here. She was the one who had been primed and readied to handle a situation like that. Courtney was not, and no matter how much Sabina loathed her, she knew she had to be cordial in this situation.

Courtney shuffled past the curtain and walked over to the other side of the bed, not looking up at Sabina for even a second, her mouth trembling, her eyes filling with tears. Sabina stepped away from Jonathan's side. Legalities aside, it was no longer her place.

Courtney looked up at. "What did the doctor say?"

"I haven't spoken to him yet."

Just then, a thirty-something man dressed in green scrubs entered the cubicle. He turned to Sabina. "Are you Mrs. Miller?"

Sabina nodded. Funny how quickly her former title had become foreign to her.

"I'm Doctor Laghari, the resident on duty. I'm sorry to say but your husband has suffered an ischemic stroke."

"What does that mean?"

"A blood clot to the brain. I understand you've signed the consent for treatment forms. We'll be taking him down for a CAT scan as soon as we can get an orderly up here, and if warranted will administer tPA, which stands for tissue plasminogen activator. Otherwise, we'll put him on blood thinners and other medications. We'll know more after the scan."

Sabina nodded, glancing over at Jonathan. "What's his prognosis?"

The doctor's gaze darted to Courtney. "Because of privacy laws—"

Sabina waved a hand in dismissal. "You can speak in front of Ms.—" Courtney's last name suddenly escaped her. "Her."

The doctor reached over and glanced at his tablet. "We've

stabilized him, he's breathing on his own, but he hasn't regained consciousness since he arrived."

"He said he felt funny and was going to go lay on the couch," Courtney volunteered and sniffled. "But he never made it there. He went down—and hard. I couldn't get him up so I called nine-one-one. He was still conscious then, but he was confused and his face was drooping on one side. He was awake until they put him in the ambulance."

The doctor looked back at them. "We'll give you an update as soon as we know what we're dealing with."

"Thank you," Sabina said.

The doctor nodded and left the women. Courtney sighed and plopped into the chair next to Jonathan's bed. Sabina turned to go when Courtney called out. "Wait! Are you going to leave me here alone with him?"

Sabina's gaze shifted to take her in, noting the look of panic on her face. "I need to see if Marisa has gotten here. I don't suppose I'll be leaving the hospital any time soon."

A tear cascaded down Courtney's left cheek and she nodded before looking away. Sabina couldn't help but notice that the woman seemed to be avoiding even looking at Jonathan. Sabina shifted her gaze to take him in. She'd been married to the man for twenty years and while she could muster sympathy for him, she felt annoyed that the man who'd abandoned her now depended upon her to make decisions concerning his health and future. Courtney had wanted to take Sabina's place in Jonathan's life, and now that she got what she wanted, was she capable of taking the bad with the good?

Sabina headed back to the waiting room. When she walked through the doors, Todd, Marisa, and Steve nervously stood. Sabina put her arms out and wrapped Marisa in a hug, kissing her forehead. Her eyes shifted to Steve's and she gave him a sweet smile. Pulling back from Marisa, Sabina wiped the streaks of tears from her daughter's face. "They believe he's had a stroke.

He's stable. They're taking him for scans. They'll let us know when they know what the damage is."

"Where's Courtney?" Marisa asked sourly.

"She's with your Dad."

Marisa scowled. "Is he talking?"

Sabina's heart skipped a beat. "No baby. He isn't conscious."

Marisa's shoulders slumped. "Can I see him?"

Sabina gave her a sweet smile. "Of course. Give me one minute to say goodbye to Steve and I'll take you back there."

Marisa moved to stand next to Todd and Sabina looked up at Steve. "Thank you for dinner, at least what we were actually able to eat."

He rested a hand on her shoulder. "We'll do another raincheck. Are you sure you don't need me to stay to make sure you guys get home later?"

Todd waved a hand in the air. "I live five minutes away. I can come grab them whenever they're ready."

Sabina nodded. "Yeah, it's okay, really. I have no idea how long we'll be here tonight. We might even be here *all* night."

Steve hugged Sabina tightly and squeezed Marisa's shoulder. "Let me know if you need a place to eat turkey on Thursday. We like company."

Sabina smiled. "Thanks."

They watched Steve leave and Todd sat down, letting Sabina know he would hang out until they knew more. She put her arm around her daughter's shoulder and led her to the reception desk to get a visitors' badge and then back through the emergency room to the curtained cubicle. That probably meant Jonathan hadn't yet been taken for his scan. They paused. "I want you to know, your Dad looks different. I don't want it to surprise you."

Marisa nodded, taking in a deep breath. Sabina pulled the curtain back and they walked in. Marisa stiffened, drawing in a sharp breath, her clenched fists flying to cover her mouth, her eyes filling with tears. She turned to Sabina and rested her face on her shoulder. Courtney had the good grace to edge past them and leave the cubicle, giving them a private moment with Jonathan. Marisa hugged her mother for a long moment before she pulled away and looked back at her father.

"Do you think he can hear us?" she asked.

Sabina shrugged. "I don't know, but it's worth a try. I'm sure the sound of your voice will comfort him."

Marisa sniffled and walked over to the bed, placing her hand on Jonathan's. It took all Sabina's resolve not to cry. Not for Jonathan, but for their daughter.

Marisa bent down to kiss her dad's cheek. "I love you, Daddy. We're here now—mom and me. We'll be here until you're well again."

A couple of orderlies in scrubs showed up with a gurney. "Ma'am, we need to take the patient to—"

"Yes," Sabina interrupted.

"You can stay here if you want," said one of the nurses behind him, "but it might take an hour or more before we bring him back."

"Thanks," Sabina said.

They watched as the orderlies moved Jonathan onto the gurney and out the double doors that led to other parts of the hospital. The doors closed automatically and Sabina turned away. Courtney stood across the way, talking on her phone, so Sabina took her daughter back to the waiting room where they joined Todd. She handed Marisa a five-dollar bill and a tissue from her purse. "Why don't you guys find us some coffee? I'm going to give Julie a call."

Marisa sniffled, took the money, and shuffled off.

"I'll take good care of her," Todd whispered and hurried to catch up with her.

Sabina retrieved her phone from her purse, took a deep breath, and walked outside, welcoming the brisk, cold air that helped sharpen her thoughts. This was not at all how she thought she'd be spending her evening. She pulled out her phone, stabbed the contacts icon, and scrolled through until she came to her best friend's number.

"I was just about to call to ask you about your date," Julie said.

"Hey," Sabina said with exhaustion.

Julie went silent for a moment. "Uh-oh, you don't sound good. What's going on? What did Jonathan do now?" she asked sarcastically.

Sabina forced a laugh. "He had a stroke."

"Oh my God! Is he all right? Do you need me to come?" Julie was always the one to volunteer to be there when anything—good or bad—happened.

Sabina began to walk along the sidewalk. "No, but thanks for offering. They're just now starting to run tests. I was having dinner with Steve when Marisa called to tell me that Courtney had contacted her. Because of HIPAA laws, Courtney couldn't authorize treatment, let alone be told his condition or prognosis. Since legally I'm still his wife, they needed me to sign the paperwork."

"Have you seen him."

"Yeah, but he wasn't conscious."

"Oh man," Julie sighed. "Are you okay? I mean, I know he's a douche bag, but he *is* your ex douche bag."

Sabina smiled. "I'm okay. I think between the last few years of our marriage, him cheating on me, and our upcoming divorce, I was right on the cusp of not caring about him. And then Friday night, when Marisa went home, things didn't turn out well." She caught Julie up with everything else that had happened.

"Yeah, how is Missy handling everything?" Julie asked.

"Better than I thought," Sabina replied. "There were tears, of course, but I just sent her to go get some coffee and we'll just have to go from there. What tragedies have befallen you guys?"

Julie groaned. "My home oven bit the dust and with the holiday season right here, I'm not going to be able to replace it until after Thanksgiving. I was hoping I could talk you into hosting us for Thanksgiving dinner if I helped cook everything."

"Well, that sucks," Sabina said and laughed. "But, you know, that might be a good idea. Of course, I don't have a lot of room, but if I know Marisa, she's going to want to spend every waking moment here with her father and that's not going to be good for her. I think having some sort of Thanksgiving dinner would be a nice break from everything. It'll also give me something else to think about. These kinds of situations can get really stressful."

"Are you sure? Because Zoey and I can go out to eat somewhere or come and have a really bad hospital food Thanksgiving dinner with you guys in the cafeteria."

Sabina flinched. "Not a chance. Let's do it. Besides, after tonight, unless I'm absolutely needed, I don't intend to spend every waking moment at Jonathan's side. He made the choice that he didn't want me around, and I've accepted it. I'll do whatever I can, or whatever I have to because I'm still legally his wife, but other than that, I have a new life of my own to lead."

As Sabina turned around to pace back toward the hospital doors, Marisa stuck her head out and waved at her mom to come inside. "I have to go. But make a list of all the things we need and we'll talk about it tomorrow, okay?"

"You got it," Julie responded. "And if Jonathan wakes up… give him the finger for me."

Sabina laughed as she ended the call, heading back into the hospital, not looking forward to the hours that lay ahead. She decided she'd try to spend the majority of her time in the ER's waiting room and let Marisa and Courtney keep a vigil. Still, as much as she disliked Jonathan, she hoped for her daughter's sake he made a full recovery.

Only time would tell.

CHAPTER 18

The next morning, Sabina stood at her kitchen counter, waiting for the kettle to boil. It had been nearly two when she and Marisa arrived back at her apartment. Marisa hadn't wanted to leave, but as her father's condition was considered stable, there really wasn't anything they could do for him. It was one of the nurses who convinced Marisa that they would take good care of her Dad and that she needed to rest and be strong for him. Sabina was grateful for her intervention. Courtney hadn't stayed as long. She'd left the hospital before midnight.

Was that the woman Jonathan wanted to spend the rest of his life with?

Good luck, buddy, Sabina thought.

Rather than yank Todd out of bed in the middle of the night, Sabina called a cab. On the ride home, Marisa kept insisting she wasn't tired, but when they got home, she took a shower and almost immediately passed out on her mom's bed.

The water boiled, and Sabina made herself a pot of tea, hoping Marisa wasn't going to expect her to spend the day at the hospital. She had plans for the week—not just for Thanksgiving, but it was a workday and she had a business to run.

In the past, hosting Thanksgiving had been a royal pain. The stress, the running around, the planning. But that year, Sabina would be happy not to have to think about her ailing almost ex for a little while.

Her phone vibrated on the counter and she picked it up, a small smile crossing her lips as she saw Steve's name flash across the screen. "Hey there."

"Hey," he replied, sounding a bit surprised. "I wasn't sure if I'd be able to get a hold of you. Are you still at the hospital?"

Sabina yawned, stretching her arms out to the sides. "No. Jonathan had tests and was still stable, so there wasn't anything that we could do. We left so Marisa could get some sleep. I'm just glad to be out of there and away from the stress of it all—at least for a while."

"Are you holding up okay?" he asked, sounding sincere.

"Yeah, I'm fine. Thanks for asking. I feel bad for my daughter. It's Missy who's kind of a mess. But I've got other things to think about. My friend Julie's oven died and now I'm in charge of hosting Thanksgiving dinner."

Steve laughed. "I was just calling you to see if you and Marisa wanted to join me and my son for Thanksgiving dinner at a restaurant. David usually spends the holidays with his mother, but this year she's on a cruise. I started looking at what I needed to do to cook Thanksgiving dinner and I panicked."

Sabina grinned, looking down at the list she'd started to make. "Well, why don't you and your son just join us for Thanksgiving? Julie, her daughter, and Marisa will be here, and I assume that Todd will be joining us, though I haven't talked to him yet."

"Of course he will," Steve said nonchalantly. "I can't tell whether he wants a job or if he wants you to adopt him."

They both laughed and it was Steve who spoke again first. "If you don't think it will be too much of an imposition, we'd love to have Thanksgiving dinner with you. I'm pretty sure my son will thank you for not forcing him to eat some wretched burnt offerings or tikka masala take-out."

"You are more than welcome. I'll be happy to have you here," she replied.

They talked for a little bit longer and then said good-bye with plans to firm up their plans on Wednesday. Sabina crossed off the number of people at the top of her list and added two more. She had exactly three days until Thanksgiving and had a lot of work to do. Glancing around the apartment, remembering how crowded it looked when both Steve and the scrawny pizza boy stood at the front door. If Steve's son was anything like him, those guys would fill up the entire living room. She definitely could not have Thanksgiving dinner at her place.

She poured herself a cup of tea, grabbed her notebook, and walked into the living room, plopping down on the couch. She knew the only other option was to host Thanksgiving dinner at her store, which didn't exactly sound cheerful at first, but thinking about the warm ambiance of the place, it was probably an even better idea than any of their homes. The store had a small but functional kitchen, and enough room to house as many people as she cared to host. Steve's son, David, would be the only one she didn't know.

"I'm hungry," a weary voice came from the hall.

Sabina looked up to find her daughter, hair a mess, and sleep in her eyes, shambling toward the kitchen. "You haven't even been asleep for nearly long enough. Are you sure you want to get up now?"

Marisa nodded, curling up on the couch next to her mom. "I was having nightmares. Then I woke up and I was hungry. What are you doing?"

Sabina held up the notebook. "Julie's oven broke and she asked me to host Thanksgiving dinner."

Marisa wrinkled her nose and glanced around the room. "Here?"

Sabina laughed. "No—at the showroom. Besides, the guest list is growing and I wouldn't be able to accommodate everyone here. It'll be you and me, Julie and Zoey, and possibly Todd. My friend and contractor Steve and his college-age son are coming, too. Apparently, Steve isn't a very good cook and I felt sorry for them."

"Do you feel sorry for Daddy?"

"I'm sorry he's not well. I hope he'll have a speedy recovery."

Marisa frowned. "Do you think maybe we should invite Courtney?"

Sabina's eyes widened and she shook her head. "I'm all about being there for you and doing what I have to do for your father, but there is a line, sweetheart. You can't believe how difficult it was for me to stand in that hospital with the woman your father cheated on me with, got her pregnant, and then sprung a divorce on me out of nowhere over breakfast. I wouldn't enjoy Thanksgiving with her at the table."

Sabina waited for Marisa to object, but her protestations didn't surface. Instead, she shrugged and nodded. "I just figured it might be nice since, you know."

"You've got a big heart, kiddo."

"Anyway, I'm pretty sure Courtney has people coming over to the house. I heard her talking about her family coming when I first came home. One of them was supposed to stay in my new room."

Sabina put her arm around Marisa's shoulder. "I'm sure your father will appreciate that you wanted to take care of Courtney during this time. But let her enjoy Thanksgiving in our old house with her family and we'll make some new traditions together. Okay?"

Marisa nodded and stood. "I guess I'd better go back to the hospital today. Will you drop me off?"

"Sure."

Marisa got up and padded back to the bedroom to change her clothes. She turned around and pointed at Sabina, thinking hard. "Actually, I just remembered, when we were waiting on dad to come back from tests, I overheard Courtney on the phone. I think she was telling her family *not* to come because of what was going on with dad."

Sabina nodded. "That's probably a good choice for her, it would be a lot of work. But as understanding and kind as I am, I'm not going to move on this one, baby."

Marisa nodded again, still not upset, which was good because Sabina wasn't up for a battle, and continued down the hall. As Sabina sipped her tea, she heard a knock on the door and rolled her eyes. Her tea would be stone-cold at this rate.

She looked out the peephole and saw Todd smiling brightly with breakfast and more coffee.

Sabina swung open the door open. "Come on in."

"You never called me last night," Todd protested.

"We decided to let you catch up on your beauty sleep."

Todd looked at himself in the mirror that hung in the entryway. "Do I look that bad?"

"No. In fact, with that bag of goodies and cups of java, you're the most handsome creature I've seen today."

"Creature?" he asked, smarting. "I'm not exactly a tarantula."

"No, you're not. Take off your coat and stay awhile."

Todd handed her the bag and did as he was told. "I started thinking about you guys, and I figured you'd probably be hungry."

Suddenly, Marisa bounded into the room. For a moment, Sabina thought Marisa was going to jump into Todd's arms, but she seemed far more interested in the breakfast sandwiches in the bag he'd brought. He grinned and winked at Sabina.

Sabina abandoned her tea and lifted the lid on her coffee

while Todd unpacked the food and tossed each of them a sandwich.

"Plates, please," Sabina chided her daughter.

Grudgingly, Marisa took out three sandwich plates, placing them on the peninsula before taking a seat and diving into her sandwich.

Sabina glanced at Todd. "What are your plans for Thanksgiving. Will you be spending it with family?"

Todd shook his head. "My parents retired to Florida. I haven't had a real Thanksgiving dinner for the past three years. Charles didn't let us have any time off for Thanksgiving, so I couldn't visit family. Last year he invited some of the associates to his house. His idea of a feast consisted of frou-frou dishes that no one wanted to eat, and then he had the gall to ask us to cough up for part of the cost."

Sabina shook her head. "Cheap bastard. Well, if you'd like, you're welcome to have dinner with us on Thanksgiving. I'm hosting it at the showroom because Julie's oven broke and this place is too small. I figured, the more the merrier."

Todd looked at Sabina, then over at Marisa. "Seriously?"

Sabina laughed. "Of course."

"Wow," he said and looked touched.

"Don't get all sappy on me. It'll be turkey, potatoes, and all the things that make you sleepy. And then there will be a lot of dishes to wash."

Todd nodded. "I can do dishes. Thanks."

Sabina tucked into her sandwich. Marisa had already finished hers and had moved on to draining her coffee cup.

"Not only am I the city's greatest breakfast fairy," Todd began and sipped his Joe, "but I have very good hearing. And it just so happens that a little birdie told me that several of Charles's clients have exchanged decorating horror stories with each other *and* an attorney."

Sabina raised an eyebrow. "Do tell."

Todd nodded. "It seems my former boss may have padded their invoices, cheating them out of thousands of dollars when he oversaw the renovations to their homes."

"In what way?"

"Well," Todd began, seeming to enjoy sharing the salacious details. "Basically, he placed fake Persian rugs and designer furniture in their homes but charged them full shot. One of the ladies spilled red wine on her rug and when she took it to an expert to be cleaned, he gave her the bad news."

"How interesting," Sabina opined.

"This could be a great opportunity for Sabina Reigns Designs to take those clients and run," Todd said coyly.

Sabina wasn't much on revenge, and truly believed that karma cut both ways, but there would be no better way to celebrate her holidays than knowing odious Charles Patterson might finally get what he deserved. That said, she wasn't going to get her hopes up. Rumors were rumors for a reason. But if what Todd said was true, she wouldn't feel all that bad about it.

CHAPTER 19

*I*n retrospect, the idea of throwing a Thanksgiving dinner on a few days' notice was pure lunacy. But then the past couple of months had been more of the same, so Sabina decided to approach the event with a sense of playfulness instead of duty. It would give her at least one day where she could let off steam and just be herself. She missed cooking for more than one and looked forward to the company. The entire situation with Jonathan had sent her spinning between a sense of duty to Marisa and a need to separate herself as much as possible from Jonathan's health crisis. Not to mention, the longer he lay there like a vegetable, the more she began to feel sorry for him.

But when she woke up on Thanksgiving morning, Sabina decided not to spend the day thinking about the man who'd done her wrong. After all, he'd decided he didn't want her in his life. Her gift had been to give him his wish. So while she got ready for the day, she made a concerted effort to enjoy the day with her daughter and some old and new friends.

Marisa had spent the previous three days at the hospital, and for most of that time, she'd been alone. Jonathan had been moved out of the ICU and into a regular room. Courtney had shown up for an hour or so in the evening, explaining that she had to be at work during the day, but the two hadn't spoken much. They just sat there in silence, while Jonathan lay in bed oblivious to them and Marisa flipped channels on the room's TV. Even so, it had taken a lot of persuasion for Sabina to talk Marisa into taking the holiday off from her vigil.

Sabina turned on the coffeemaker and poked at her daughter, ignoring her groans and attitude, but Marisa eventually sat up, which was a start.

Standing in the kitchen, Sabina retrieved a couple of mugs from the cupboard and watched as Marisa stumbled off the couch, rubbing her stiff neck. "Good morning, sunshine."

Marisa glanced up at her mother with a sneer. "Why are you so grossly happy at this time of the morning?"

Again, Sabina ignored her daughter's foul mood. "It's Thanksgiving. We're going to have some yummy food, spend time with friends, and relax. And the parade is about to start on television."

Marisa rolled her eyes. "Mom, I'm not ten anymore."

Turning, Sabina poured her daughter a cup of coffee, smiling to herself as she heard Marisa turn on the TV and flip the channel to the parade. When she turned back around, Marisa shook her head and scowled. "Not a word."

Sabina threw her hands up in surrender and tried to hide a smirk. She took Marisa her coffee and sat down next to her, silently pleased with the idea of just hanging out with her not-so-little girl doing something they'd always done in the past. Marisa shrieked with glee at the enormous Snoopy float that moved down Broadway despite the high winds in New York that day. But as the laughter faded, Marisa let out a deep sigh. "I miss Dad. I was just about to turn to him to watch him do that Cookie Monster impression he used to do."

Sabina laughed, the joy in it catching her by surprise. "I nearly forgot about that. He would make a mess, grabbing whatever was in front of him and smash it against his face."

They both giggled and Marisa shrugged. "See? Being with dad wasn't *all* bad."

Sabina blinked in surprise, realizing that maybe she'd been so caught up in her own hurt that lately she'd portrayed their lives as always being hopeless and loveless. She didn't want Marisa to forget that they had once been a family, however dysfunctional.

She sat her coffee on the side table and reached over, taking Marisa's hands in hers. "Baby, I never meant to make you feel as though I never loved your father. We were best friends for a very long time. I have a lot of good memories of him, but things changed between us these past five or so years."

"Maybe he was just going through a mid-life crisis. Maybe things won't work out with Courtney and you two can get back together," Marisa said, her voice filled with hope.

"It doesn't work that way, honey. Besides, Courtney wasn't his first fling."

"Oh," Marisa said sadly.

"But the best thing that ever came from our marriage was you. I know this is terribly hard for you, and I'm so sorry you have to see your dad so sick in the hospital. But I want you to know that I'll love you forever, and despite his recent behavior, I know your dad will, too."

Marisa stared down at their hands and nodded. "I know. I feel bad when I lose my temper and yell at you. I'm going to work on that. I promise."

Sabina smiled and leaned forward, kissing her daughter on the top of her head.

Marisa suddenly jumped up and headed for the bedroom. "I'm gonna take a shower, eat, and then we can head over to the show-room, okay?"

"That's the plan."

After showers and several of what Sabina joked as costume changes, mom and daughter headed over to the shop. No one else was there when they arrived at the nearly empty plaza, so they lugged the bags of food inside and into the kitchen. As Sabina began unloading, Marisa glanced around the showroom. "Do you mind if I try to make the showroom a little homier?"

"Trying to upstage your mother?"

Marisa smiled shyly. "Nah. But I was thinking I might work on my dorm room when I go back to school. This will give me some practice."

"Sure, baby. Anything you want."

"Great. I promise, to put everything back by tomorrow," she said, but before she could head off, Sabina spoke again.

"Hey, Missy, could you make a point of being extra nice to Zoey today? She and Aunt Julie have been going through a rough time lately."

"I got that impression on Friday night."

"Right about now, Zoey could use a friend."

"That's me," Marisa said and off she went into the showroom.

Sabina allowed herself a smile. God, she loved her kid.

As Sabina stocked the fridge, she allowed herself a smile. Maybe one day she'd change the name of the business to Designs by Sabina Reigns & Daughter. One of their favorite things to do in years past was to decorate the house for the holidays over Thanksgiving weekend. They went all out spreading holiday cheer through every room in the house. It wouldn't take long to decorate the tiny apartment. Worst of all, Courtney was now in possession of all of the family's decorations.

Still, Black Friday was only hours away and because of the sales, they could probably do a lot for a little. It might be fun to hit up a few craft stores and decorate the small apartment. It would make the place a lot more cheerful and Sabina would need that after Marisa returned to school. Two and a half days—that's all Sabina had before she was alone once again. And if Jonathan's condition deteriorated would Marisa sacrifice her first semester at Carnegie Mellon U? Sabina crossed her fingers. That rat-bastard of a husband of hers had better recover if only for his daughter's sake.

* * *

TODD WAS the first of the crew to arrive at the showroom. A muffled pounding on the plate glass was Sabina's first clue. There he stood, surrounded by bags and boxes, dressed in Dockers, a bulky sweater, and leather boots looking stylish and, dare she say it, rather hunky? The multicolored hand-knit ski hat atop his head seemed out of phase with his usual GQ image, but he looked happy and comfortable. Sabina wanted everyone to be comfortable.

"Happy Thanksgiving," Sabina called and smiled as she helped him in with his bags. "I told you that you didn't need to bring anything."

Todd scoffed. "Girl, please. I brought cheese, wine, fruit platters, and dips. The whole nine yards. You know how people are on Thanksgiving, they're starving as soon as they wake up."

Sabina grinned, turning to walk to the kitchen. Just as they did, the bell on the door rang again and she looked over her shoulder to see Steve and his son, who was as tall and good looking as his father, walk in. They each carried boxes filled with liquor.

Todd stifled a laugh and took the bags from Sabina. "Go greet your man."

Sabina gave him a look and handed the rest over, straightening her sweater as she walked toward them. Steve grinned and leaned over, kissing Sabina on the cheek. "Wow, it looks like a party is about to happen."

Sabina opened the turned-in flap on the box and gaped. "Wow. Do you think we're all a bunch of lushes?"

Steve laughed. "What kind of Thanksgiving would it be if

someone wasn't passed out from too much whiskey in the eggnog. Minus the eggnog."

Steve's son politely smiled and Sabina jumped, leading him over to the front counter and pushing several papers aside. "Here, just put those down here. We'll get it all set up."

She stood back as they put the boxes on the counter and they turned back to her. Steve slapped his son on the shoulder. "This is my son, David."

Sabina reached out and shook his hand. "Nice to meet you, David. I'm Sabina, that was my friend and assistant, Todd, and my daughter Marisa is around here somewhere."

"Right here," Marisa said as she hopped up next to her mother. She put out her hand toward David. "Hey."

"Hey yourself," he replied with a shy grin.

Sabina narrowed her eyes at the two as they stared a bit too long at each other. "Okay. Why don't you take David's and Steve's coats and show them where they can settle down and relax? I am going to continue unpacking food so Julie doesn't kill me when she gets here. Luckily, she bought a cooked and ready-to-go turkey so that won't take too long to reheat. We just have to make the rest of the sides."

"Do you need some help?" Steve asked.

Sabina shook her head. "No, no. Go relax, play with the television, I haven't really tried out the streaming service yet. I'm sure there's football on some channel."

He smiled. "Thanks. If you need help with anything, just yell."

"Gobble, gobble," Julie hollered as she walked in the door carrying several bags.

Zoey struggled in behind her, a bit of a wobble in her step as she carried a box topped off with marshmallows and cocoa. Sabina hurried over to help, despite Julie's side glance and took the box from Zoey, giving her a wink as she took it. "Why don't you go hang out with Marisa. With all that's happened with her dad, I'm betting she could use a friendly face."

Zoey smiled and hurried off before Julie had time to chastise her daughter.

As Julie and Sabina cooked, trading good-natured barbs, Sabina took a moment to sneak a look into the showroom to see that Zoey and Marisa were seated in the elegant living room, snacking and gossiping. They were only three years apart in age and Zoey had looked up to Marisa like the big sister she never had.

David, Steve, and Todd sat in the farmhouse living room, this one more suited for comfort, and watched football on the big screen television Sabina had splurged on for the showroom. It was also the one she planned to liberate from the shop and put in her new house one day in what now seemed like the distant future.

With the turkey in the oven, and the vegetables all set to go, Sabina readied a tray full of rolls to toss in whenever there was room. Julie peeked out the door to the showroom beyond. Sabina raised a brow as she set the tray down. "Is everyone out there still alive?"

Julie wiped her hands on a towel and nodded toward the others. "Have you ever seen a gay man enjoy football so much?"

Sabina strained to look around the corner to where Steve, David, and Todd sat, entranced in front of the boob tube. "I'm sure loads of gay guys watch sports. I mean, let's face it. Some of the players are real attractive hunks."

Julie shook her head, suspicion clouding her features. "Yeah, and most of them are nothing but muscle and bone on steroids. But he doesn't seem to be admiring them in that way. And have you seen the furtive glances he gives Marisa when he thinks no one's looking?"

Sabina glanced through the doorway at Todd, whose attention seemed to be focused on the television, not on her daughter. "No. Besides, he straight up told me he was gay."

145

Julie looked down at Sabina. "And if I told you I was the Queen of England, would you believe me, too?"

Sabina stood straighter and headed back for the oven. "Just make the gravy."

She didn't want to think about it. She'd seen Marisa making googly eyes in David's direction and death stares at Steve. The idea that her gay assistant might not actually be gay was ludicrous. She turned her thoughts back into her happy holiday place, hummed "Jingle Bells," and took the butter dish out to the counter that would act as a buffet.

After setting it down, she noticed that while Marisa had joined the nacho-snacking guys in the south side of the pseudo living room, Zoey remained alone in the north side of the room scrolling through her phone, looking rather desolate.

Julie came up from behind her with a bowl of cranberry sauce. Don't feel sorry for her," she warned.

Sabina turned. "What do you mean?"

"Zoey got herself in trouble. She has to live with the consequences."

Sabina's gaze wandered back to the girl, her heart sinking. Julie was handling the situation all wrong. Okay, she was disappointed. Nobody wants their child to put limitations on their future—and giving birth at fifteen was one hell of a limitation, but Zoey was still just a kid. And Sabina had no doubt that when the baby arrived, Julie's heart would melt and she would support her daughter—emotionally and financially—and love that little bundle of joy. If only Sabina could talk to Julie about it, but it was one subject Julie would not discuss—and probably because she knew what Sabina's pitch would be and she wasn't in a place where she could hear it.

Yet.

"I think I'll go talk to her," Sabina said.

"Don't expect to get much more than a few grunts. That's all I get from her these days."

Sabina shrugged. "Maybe I'll do better."

"Good luck."

Sabina picked up a bowl of M&Ms and headed across the showroom.

"Hey, Zoey, all the snacks are with the guys across the way. Why don't you join them and Missy?"

"I'm okay where I am."

Sabina offered the candy. "I thought you might want a treat."

Zoey looked at her belly and seemed to shrink further into the couch. "Chocolate makes you fat, and I'm fat enough already."

Wow, Sabina hadn't expected the girl to be so negative. She sat next to Zoey on the couch. "We haven't had a chance to talk in a while."

"Yeah, well...you've been busy starting your business."

"I have," Sabina admitted, "but it seems like you've been hiding from me, too."

"Not really. I just ... I don't need any more lectures. I get enough of them from my mom."

"Oh, honey, I don't want to lecture you. What I do want you to know is that if you need someone to talk to, you can count on me. I promise I won't judge you."

A chorus of boos and cheers erupted from the gang in front of the tube causing Zoey to look in their direction wistfully.

"Why don't you go watch the game with Missy and the guys?" Sabina again suggested.

Zoey shrugged. "I don't like sports."

"What do you like?"

"Nothing." Zoey's tone was just so flat—so *dead*.

Sabina tried another tack. "Have you decided on a name?"

Zoey frowned. "A name?"

"For your baby?"

Zoey shook her head. "I was thinking of calling her It. I mean, my mom says I can't keep her. I don't have any money or anywhere to go. I don't want to get too attached."

Sabina's stomach did a flip-flop as she remembered how thrilled she was to welcome Marisa to the world. Oh, sure having a baby put her career on hold for eighteen years, but she wouldn't have had it any other way...despite the more recent teenage sass.

"Have you talked to an adoption agency?" Sabina asked.

Zoey shook her head. "I was thinking about foster care, that way when I'm older I can get her back."

"Oh, Zoey," Sabina said, her heart breaking.

"But then I decided not to do that because...you know, you hear all these stories about people being mean to little kids in the system—and then there are all those sexual predators. I don't want anything bad to happen to my little girl."

"You could get help from the baby's father. It takes two to tango, as they say. As her father, he should pay child support. And if he's too young, his family should kick in. A judge could make that happen."

Zoey shook her head. "I don't want to go that route. It just wouldn't work out." Which made Sabina believe the worst about just how Zoey became pregnant in the first place.

"You've got some hard decisions ahead of you."

"Sometimes ..." Zoey stopped and sniffed. "Sometimes I just wish I'd die and then I wouldn't have to think about all this serious grown-up bullshit."

"Oh, don't say that."

Zoey shrugged. "Why not? It's true."

Sabina threw her arms around the girl and pulled her close, not knowing what to say to ease her pain. "It'll work out," she finally said. But Zoey didn't hug her back. She sat there as stiff as a mannequin. "Things have a way of working out."

"Promise?" Zoey whispered.

Sabina sighed. "Not always the way we want, but yes...things work out."

Suddenly, Zoey's arms tightened around Sabina's shoulders. "Robin," she said breathlessly. "My baby's name is Robin."

"It's a beautiful name. How did you come up with it?"

"Because robins bring hope that winter and all the gloom it brings is finally over and you can be happy again."

"Yes," Sabina agreed. "It certainly does."

"Hey, Sabina!" Julie called. "These potatoes aren't going to mash themselves".

Zoey pulled back, her cheeks pink, looking embarrassed.

"Coming," Sabina said. She patted Zoey's arm. "Remember, if you need to talk…"

"Thanks, Aunt Sabina," Zoey said and wiped at her watery eyes.

"Anytime, kiddo."

Sabina returned to the small kitchen to prepare the potatoes, but her hands were shaking as she drained the water from the pot, then took out the milk and butter. She needed to talk to Julie about Zoey but now wasn't the time. Not when they had guests. Could Zoey really be having suicidal thoughts? It was something that needed to be addressed and pretty damn quick.

It was halftime by the time the table was set, and the rest of the food was sprawled out on the shop's counter, looking like a smorgasbord. The starving horde grabbed plates and filled them, taking seats at the table in the faux dining room that Marisa had set earlier in the day. Steve poured wine for those over twenty-one and sparkling grape juice for those who weren't of age.

"Shall we have a toast?" he asked, raising his glass.

Sabina raised hers. "To happiness."

"And may we all get what we want for Christmas," Todd chimed in.

"What's that?" David asked.

"Full-time employment," he said, staring at Sabina and waggling his eyebrows.

The guys laughed and joked throughout the meal, with Julie and Marisa joining in. Every time Sabina caught sight of Zoey, she flashed what she hoped was an encouraging smile.

At one-point, Sabina sat back listening to the camaraderie, realizing how lucky she was to have assembled her own little misfit family. This holiday was definitely different than Thanksgivings of the past.

They'd missed the beginning of the third quarter, and Sabina and Julie assured the guys—and girls—that they could handle the cleanup. It would give Sabina the opportunity to speak to Julie alone.

She cleared her throat as she rinsed the plates, handing them to Julie to load into the small dishwasher. "Thanks for doing this with us."

Julie sipped her wine. "Pfft, thank you for rescuing Thanksgiving. My oven tried to thwart me with its evil ways but we were smarter."

"Yeah. Just like grownups," Sabina replied feeling her gut tightening.

Julie gulped the rest of her wine. "Speak for yourself hussy. I am forever young." She laughed, but Sabina couldn't muster a smile.

"Jules, I need to talk to you about something important."

"And ruin our great day? This meal was such an outstanding success, I intend to celebrate it until Christmas."

"Yeah, we always have worked well together."

A cheer rang out from the front of the shop—another touchdown, no doubt.

"We didn't burn anything or anyone, none of the kids have fought yet, and everyone is happy. That's the best we could ask for."

"Well, not everyone is happy."

"Oh, yeah. Well, Miss Mar-iss was bound to be unhappy what with her dad in the hospital, but she bucked up."

"I'm not talking about her. I'm talking about Zoey."

Julie waved a hand in dismissal. "She's just sulking."

"I think it's a little more than sulking. She told me she wishes she was dead."

The merriment drained from Julie's face. "No. I don't believe it. She's just trying to get attention."

"And what if she isn't?"

Julie's mouth flattened into a thin line. She marched over the to counter and poured another glass of wine, taking a deep gulp. "Why'd you have to ruin my day? I haven't had a good day since—"

"Since you found out your daughter was pregnant?"

"Yes."

"I don't think she's had a good day, either. All you guys have done is fight about the future—not discuss what's going to happen in another three or four weeks. Have you listened to what she wants to do?"

"She wants to keep that baby and she can't. I can't. I work like a dog and am just eking out a living. I can't afford another mouth to feed, let alone pay for daycare. If she keeps that baby—"

"Her name is Robin."

Julie let out a breath. "She told you that?"

Sabina nodded.

Julie shook her head, her gaze focused on the tile floor. "If Zoey keeps that baby her life will be ruined. She'll never go to college. She'll never have a decent-paying job—"

"You're not giving her much credit."

"She's a kid. She doesn't have a clue what bringing up a child entails."

"You ever heard of on-the-job training?" Sabina suggested.

"Don't be funny."

"I wasn't trying to be."

Julie kept shaking her head.

"At least have her talk to a therapist."

"Yeah, and where's the money going to come for that?"

"Ask her obstetrician. Maybe she can line her up with

someone to talk to—or ask her to talk to Zoey herself. She must come across this kind of situation all the time."

Julie let out a breath. "Okay. I'll call the office tomorrow, and if they're not open tomorrow, Monday."

"Thanks."

"What are you thanking me for," Julie muttered. "I suppose I should be thanking you. I'm so fucking angry with her—"

"Yeah, and she knows it. Now you've got to convince her that you still love her."

Again Julie shook her head. "You think you're so damn smart, don't you?"

"Well, yeah. I do," Sabina deadpanned.

For a moment, Julie looked like she wanted to smack her best friend, but then she threw her arms around her. "I hate you right now."

"Yeah, but you'll love me again tomorrow."

"Yeah, I probably will."

Sabina patted Julie's back and then pulled away. "We'd better get back to finishing up these dishes. They're not going to wash themselves."

"$\mathcal{A}$re you sure you have everything?" Sabina asked her daughter as they stood in front of the security gate at the Greater Rochester International Airport.

"Yes, Mom," Marisa said, sounding bored. "You will check on Dad every day, won't you?" she asked.

Sabina let out a heavy breath. "Yes, of course."

"And you'll call or text me about his condition every day, too, right?"

"Yes, I will." Sabina had only had to make that promise about a dozen times just that morning.

Marisa smiled and rolled her eyes at the same time. "Mom, I'm only going to be gone for a couple of weeks. Just make sure you check on Dad and make sure Courtney is taking care of the baby and being somewhat sane. And if Dad comes to, please tell him I love him and I'll be back soon."

"I will, baby. Now you try to push all that to the back of your mind if you can," Sabina told her as she kissed Marisa's forehead. "Just focus on getting through those exams, acing them, and then you'll be back home. We're going to have a good Christmas no matter what."

"My Christmas wish is for Dad to get better," Marisa said.

"Mine, too," Sabina said. She wasn't lying, either. "Now, you be safe and call or text me the minute you land."

Marisa nodded, her expression only hinting at how much she'd prefer to stay in a town she'd been so eager to leave back in September. Sabina didn't say anything to acknowledge that, though. She knew it was good for Marisa to get away—go back to school and hopefully not dwell on the fact her father might be a vegetable for the rest of his life. Sabina wanted her daughter to succeed no matter what happened to her father.

When Marisa had passed through the security check and was out of sight, Sabina headed back to her car. She felt that familiar feeling of being somewhat less whole without her daughter around. Of course, all she had to do was remember how much Marisa usually despised her in her young adult hormonal way, and the feeling lessened a bit.

On the way back to the apartment, Sabina decided to divert and check in on Jonathan at the hospital. She hadn't been there since before Thanksgiving and there was an annoying pull of guilt simmering in her stomach. She figured she could get in and out, make sure there was nothing she needed to do, and get back home to plan the rest of her workweek. She needed to connect with the people who'd attended her party the week before and hopefully, some of them would hire her before or just after the new year. Of course, that was always the plan but she knew things seldom ever happened that way.

She headed toward the hospital and parked her car in the big ramp garage—knowing she'd be gouged for the pleasure. Across the street was the famous Victorian cemetery known as Mount Hope, where it was said the doctors buried their mistakes. She didn't find the old saw all that funny.

As soon as Sabina stepped off the elevator, she could feel a sense of tension in the air. Within seconds, she saw Courtney, pacing back and forth the wing's waiting area, one hand pressed on her expanding belly, a look of irritation, fear, and anxiety fighting for prominence in her expression. Sabina hoped they would curtly nod at each other and Sabina would head back to Jonathan's room, but she was taken aback when their eyes met and Courtney came storming toward her.

"This is ridiculous," Courtney said, throwing her hands into the air. "I can't even sit in there with the father of my child."

Sabina glanced around. "What's going on? I told them you have permission to visit whenever you want."

"Yeah," she scoffed. "Except they don't like me. They don't care who I am. They ignore me when I tell them something needs to be done, and Jonathan isn't improving at all. I feel like I'm all alone in this whole damn thing. He loves *me*, but you've got all the power."

Sabina raised an eyebrow but bit her tongue. No matter how she felt about Courtney, no matter how much of a home-wrecker the woman was, Courtney was little more than a scared girl. Carrying on with an older man had plenty of perks—especially financially, but Courtney had probably never given a second thought that an older man might be prone to health problems. Jonathan was only forty-five. Even Sabina would have never imagined he'd have a stroke at such a young age. And here was Courtney, pregnant, alone, and with (hopefully) no legal rights to anything Jonathan owned, watching the man she depended on wasting away in a hospital bed.

Sabina wasn't sure she had any words of comfort to share with the woman in front of her. Her silence only seemed to anger Jonathan's mistress more.

"This is pointless," Courtney cried in frustration. "You know what? I'm just going to go home."

Whose home? Sabina's name was still on the deed.

Sabina watched as Courtney grabbed her coat, walked past her, and stabbed the elevator button. Her exit would have been far more dramatic if the elevator's doors had immediately opened to hasten her escape. To spare her more embarrassment, Sabina turned and headed toward the wing's nurses' desk. Standing behind the counter was a middle-aged nurse, the skin around her eyes lined, looking worn out. How long had she been on duty? "Can I help you?"

"I'm Sabina Reigns Miller. Jonathan Miller's wife."

The nurse blew out a breath and sighed. "By any chance is there some way you can curtail Ms. Sullivan's visits?"

Sabina gave her a look of pity and frowned. "What's she done?"

"For one, she doesn't seem to understand HIPAA rules. When we try to explain them, she loses her temper. We've had to ask her to leave the unit several times and even threatened to call security if she didn't calm down."

"Is she really that bad?"

"Today she was," the nurse said wearily. "It's usually the night crew she menaces, but today… When she's here, she gets angry that Mr. Miller won't respond to her. She's rude to the nurses and tends to yell at us in front of Mr. Miller. It's not healthy for him to be exposed to all of that."

"I'm sorry. I wish there was something I could do to remedy the situation, but she's angry at me, too. For what it's worth, I don't think she'll be around all that much, which is sad in some ways since she is carrying his child."

The nurse shook her head. "That's got to be hard for you."

"It is, but I need to take the high ground, if only for our daughter's sake. Can you give me an update on his condition?

"I'm sorry to say it hasn't changed since he was brought down here on Friday. As per the attending physician's instructions, we did go ahead and insert the feeding tube."

Sabina nodded. "I understand. Thanks."

"Is there anything else you need?" the nurse inquired sincerely.

Sabina offered a wan smile. "I'll let you know after I see him. Thanks."

The nurse gave her a sympathetic smile and Sabina made her way to Jonathan's private room, which had to be costing a mint. The monitors were gone as his condition remained stable, with only the oxygen tube from the wall attached to his nose. She stepped over to the side of the bed and stared at him silently for a moment. His eyes were closed as though asleep. His mouth hung partly open, the left side of his face drooped, and his breathing was loud. He didn't look like the Jonathan she had known and once loved. If he recovered, would he be able to tap into his once-brilliant legal mind again?

Sabina set her purse on the floor and straightened the covers on the bed, tossed away a coffee cup that she assumed Courtney had left behind, and turned the volume down on the television. Jonathan hated a blaring TV and would never have watched the HGTV network. Sabina could tell from just their meeting in the waiting room that Courtney's feelings for Jonathan were already ebbing, but that wasn't Sabina's problem, at least not when it came to their relationship.

What was her problem? Was it the fact that Courtney was still staying in the house that Sabina's name was still attached to or that with Jonathan incapacitated all their lives were on hold? Maybe.

Sabina knew Courtney was spending less time with Jonathan, and as time wore on would probably soon curtail her visits even more. Added to that, she hadn't mentioned when or *if* she was going to move out of the house. It was obvious to Sabina that Jonathan wasn't going to recover anytime soon. Her grandfather had had a stroke when she was eleven and although he eventually was well enough to come home, he suffered from aphasia and wasn't able to speak and always walked with a cane. Even if Jonathan woke up that very hour, it was likely he'd have a long convalescence ahead of him.

Sabina put the thought out of her mind. And if he never was well enough to go home, should she kick Courtney out of the house? And how would it look to evict Jonathan's pregnant girlfriend? She didn't care, but perhaps some of her clients might. And if Courtney did move out, she could still sue for child support. Eighteen years was a long time to support Jonathan's love child.

A noise at the door caused Sabina to look up as a man in a white lab coat entered the room. "Hello. Are you Mrs. Miller?"

Sabina nodded.

"I'm Dr. Lewis. I'm the resident on duty."

"Hello. Sorry I haven't made it here more often." She nodded toward Jonathan. "Our daughter went back to college today, and what with the holidays, it's all been a big, complicated mess," Sabina explained, hoping he didn't ask about their personal circumstances. "Is there anything new to report?"

The doctor stared down at the tablet in his hands. "No. His vitals are stable, we put the feeding tube in to help keep him strong, but there's been no discernible change in his state of consciousness." He set the tablet on the bedside table, crossing his arms across his chest, his expression grim. "It's been a week and your husband has shown no improvement. I'm sorry to say it's time to start thinking about other options."

Was that his opinion or that of their insurance company?

"By options are you talking about transferring him to a nursing home?"

The doctor nodded. "They can do all the things that the nurses here can do, and probably more because they offer physical and occupational therapy."

Sabina cringed at the thought. You put parents in senior care, not husbands. "I understand. Thank you."

Why was she saying thank you? The last thing Sabina wanted to do was deal with a nursing home.

"Perfect," the doctor replied. "We have your contact information; one of our social workers will be in touch with you tomorrow."

"Okay," Sabina said. What else *could* she say?

The doctor gave her a nod and exited the room.

She swallowed and stared at Jonathan for a long few minutes before leaving the hospital. What was she going to tell Marisa that night? Sorry, honey, but the hospital has given up on your dad and I'm sticking him in a nursing home? Would that news cause the girl to hop on the next plane back to Rochester?

Nope. Wasn't going to happen.

If she had to, Sabina would keep telling her daughter that her father was stable, with not much in the way of improvement, because no matter what bed Jonathan occupied, it would be the truth. After Missy finished her exams, then Sabina would tell her. Yeah, it was the same kind of lie that Jonathan had told her about the divorce, but it really was for the greater good. Marisa could decide in January if she wanted to continue her freshman year at Carnegie Mellon. Ha! Maybe once she looked at the financials Sabina might not be able to send her to that pricey school and she'd have to settle for something much closer to home. There wasn't time to apply to a local college before the second semester. Maybe Marisa would have a half-gap year.

With too much on her mind, Sabina forgot where she parked her car and found herself wandering around the hospital's parking garage looking for it, growing more frustrated by the minute.

Fifteen minutes later, she got in her car and pulled out her phone, quickly searching to see what the average price per year was for the area's nursing homes. She sucked in a breath as Google delivered the bad news.

And then she thought of something else. As far as she knew Jonathan had not changed his will. She certainly hadn't changed hers and it was something she needed to do PDQ. Since she had control of Jonathan's medical needs, she might still have his power of attorney. He had emptied out their accounts, but he'd have to have opened new ones, and hopefully, in the same bank branch they'd always dealt with. Now she just had to hope he hadn't put Courtney on those accounts.

First thing in the morning she would call her attorney to make sure.

Maybe Monday would be a much, much better day after all.

* * *

SABINA DIDN'T BOTHER CALLING Marisa that evening, sending a text instead. She got a brief *Thanks, Mom,* in return.

The next morning, Sabina decided not to call to make an appointment with her lawyer and showed up at the office at precisely nine o'clock, hoping Tonya didn't have a meeting first thing with anyone else—or that she was in court. Either way, Sabina was prepared to wait—or at least come back. She wanted some assurance that she could go ahead with the plans she'd made the night before.

Sabina left her car and headed for the front door of what had once been a family home, but now was the law offices of her attorney, Tonya Harbor, and another attorney named Fred Conrad. They shared a secretary and office equipment, which meant they got to keep more of their earnings than spending big bucks for a swanky office downtown. But just because she was located in the burbs didn't mean that Tonya was a hack when it came to the law. She'd been the smartest kid in all the years they'd been in school together and was voted most likely to succeed.

"Good morning," the older woman parked at the secretary's station said with a smile. "What can I help you with?" She was not the bimbo who'd answered the phone the last time she'd called.

"Hi," Sabina replied softly. "I don't have an appointment, but I figured I would stop by and see if my attorney, Tonya, had just a few minutes to talk to me."

"I'll check for you," the woman said. "Just have a seat."

Sabina walked gingerly over and sat down on the edge of a chair, looking around. In moments, Tonya's voice rang out from the office to her right. "Sabina? Is everything all right?"

The secretary returned. "Go right in."

Sabina scooted into Tonya's office, closing the door behind her.

"It really depends on your definition of everything," Sabina lightly joked and took a seat in front of Tonya's desk. "Jonathan had a stroke right before Thanksgiving and is in the hospital unconscious."

Tonya looked at her with wide eyes. "Oh lord, that is a mess."

"Yeah." Sabina rummaged around in her big purse. "I brought a copy of our wills and health proxies. They were made up by someone in Jonathan's firm," she explained needlessly. "The hospital had no problem with me making decisions on Jonathan's behalf. What I want you to confirm is if I have his power of attorney." She handed the paperwork to the attorney.

Tonya donned a pair of reading glasses and shuffled through the pages, giving them a cursory scan. "Pretty standard stuff," she said, nodding. She read a few more paragraphs and when she looked up, she sported what could only be described as a shit-eating grin.

"Did Jonathan ever transfer those funds back into your joint accounts?"

Sabina shook her head.

"You should have come to me before this so we could have forced his hand. But that's moot now. With this sheet of paper, you can do what you want with every single nickel the bastard took from you."

Sabina let out a breath. "I was hoping you'd say that, but only because there are bills to be paid. The mortgage," which should have been paid off long before this, "and Marisa's tuition next month."

"Is the girlfriend still in your house?"

Sabina nodded.

"An accountant would tell you to pay off that mortgage ASAP, but you might want to hold off until you can get her out of there."

"I'm worried she's going to sue for child support."

"And you can request a DNA sample from the baby to prove it's Jonathan's. I would insist on it."

It hadn't occurred to Sabina that the baby might not be Jonathan's.

"What about the house?"

"That's a little more difficult," Tonya said and sat back in her big leather chair. "You still own half of the house. The problem is, from a legal standpoint, you knowingly allowed Courtney to live there. If she's done any renovations—"

"She has."

"And if any of the utilities are in her name, a judge might interpret that you've given her some kind of tenancy. Your best bet is to take her to court to evict her."

"What if Jonathan recovers?"

"It's a chance you'll have to take. What's his condition?"

"Not looking good."

"It's up to you. Legally, you call all the shots."

Sabina bit the inside of her cheek, unsure if she even wanted the house back at that point. Taking possession of it once again would make things easier for Marisa, but Sabina still had four months left on her sub-let. At the same time, could she evict a pregnant woman whose child's father was lying dormant in a hospital bed? It wasn't the type of lesson in kindness she wanted to teach her daughter.

"That's good to know," Sabina replied. "For now, I think I'll wait on eviction. Things are still early in Jonathan's recovery and honestly, from the way Courtney's been behaving, she may eventually leave on her own. But I'll keep it in the back of my mind."

"Keep me posted," Tonya said. "I'm sorry Jonathan had a

stroke. I never liked the son of a bitch, but I'd never wish that on anyone."

"Thanks," Sabina replied, giving a half-smile. "And thanks for seeing me."

"All part of the service."

Sabina left the attorney's office feeling at odds with her conscience. On one hand, she had the ability to financially care for Jonathan now that she knew she could access the accounts. On the other hand, she felt trapped in the idea that she would be the one to take care of him. And what about the divorce? She shook the thoughts from her mind, knowing everything would eventually become clear. She still had a business to run, and on top of all of that, the Park Manor Renovation was coming up. Suddenly the idea of running her business, taking care of the house, and possibly supporting two other people felt daunting and impossible to manage.

How in God's name was she going to be able to pull all that off?

CHAPTER 21

$\mathcal{A}$fter calling Todd to tell him she wouldn't be working that day, Sabina asked if he'd mind going in and manning the phones at the showroom—just in case anyone needed to book her design services.

"Anything you need, boss."

She cringed at the title. After all, it had been longer than a week and she still hadn't added him to the Sabina Reigns Designs payroll.

Sabina spent the rest of Cyber Monday talking to her accountant and dealing with banking officials, waving her power of attorney so that she once again had full access to the funds that were rightly hers in a community property state. When (or if) Jonathan recovered, they could start the separation proceedings once again—she was adamant about that.

According to the accountant, their finances were in good standing and she should be able to pay most of the bills without touching their retirement funds, but she needed to get her business truly up and running to stay ahead of the game.

In addition, she went online and found that she could download the forms to formally change her name. It would take some time, and a hellish amount of paperwork, but it was doable. In the interim, she would continue to call herself Sabina Reigns Miller for official documents, and Sabina Reigns to her new customer base. It worked for John Cougar Mellencamp—it could work for her, too.

The next morning, just before she was leaving for her showroom, Sabina received a text from Julie.

Lunch and Christmas shopping today?

Sabina had already blown off a day at work, but after their conversation four days before, she was eager to hear how Zoey was making out.

Sure. Where and when?

They decided to meet at the mall out in Greece near the food court around noon.

Sabina arrived at the showroom at nine only to find Todd was already there. A plate of croissants sat on the faux dining room's table and he'd made a fresh pot of coffee.

"You're spoiling me," Sabina exclaimed as Todd pulled out a chair for her at the head of the table.

"All part of my fiendish plan to get you to hire me. But let's not talk business just yet," he said, taking a seat at her right. He poured coffee for them both and encouraged her to take one of the croissants. A small ramekin of whipped butter and some kind of jam in an identical container awaited. She tore off a piece of her roll and smeared the end of it with both before taking a bite. "Raspberry jam is my favorite. How did you know?"

Todd shrugged. "A little birdie told me."

Is she five foot five and as cute as a button?"

"She might be," he admitted. He took a sip of coffee. "I have some absolutely delicious gossip to pass on. That is if you're interested in listening."

"That depends on the subject."

"My former employer," Todd said and took a bite of his breakfast, too.

"Does it reinforce what you've already told me?"

Todd leaned closer. "In spades," he said gleefully.

"Then spill all."

It took him only a minute to bring her up to date.

"So then, she flipped over one of the cushions, cut it open with a knife, and found it stuffed with the grimiest synthetic fibers," Todd explained. "We're talking oily rags contaminated with who knows what—the worst of the worst from a third-world country."

Sabina shook her head. "What a joke. And to think Patterson had the nerve to walk around my new showroom, acting like a complete—well, you know what he acted like. And the whole time he was pulling a con on his clients. He was conning everyone."

Todd nodded, swallowing a bite of croissant. "I can almost hear the sound of fake high-end upholstery being ripped all over the region. And the news spread really fast. Word has it that darling Charles has no clients left. They're all looking for somebody to fix what they're now suing him over. So, I figured, this might be a good time to reach out to some of your old contacts from the time you worked for him."

"Those who aren't dead," Sabina said with a shake of her head.

"They trust you. They know you. And you could easily be booked for the next two years."

Sabina took in a deep breath. While it was exciting to contemplate, and good for her business, not to mention very satisfying considering how shabbily Charles Patterson had always treated her, it was also overwhelming.

"That brings me to one specific order of business that we haven't yet discussed," she began.

"You look awfully serious."

"It's time. As you know, the Park Manor project is about to go into full swing and we have tons of work to do to make sketches and mockups for the board who'll decide what they want us to implement during the renovation. On top of that, we have a host of potential clients we assume will soon be knocking on our doors. Right now, it's just me. Your free trial is over, though I do appreciate you not bringing it up until I had a chance to collect myself."

Todd put down his croissant and wiped his mouth with a napkin, looking quintessentially professional. "And have you figured anything out?"

Sabina bit the inside of her cheek. "I think so, at least for now. Having Jonathan's power of attorney gives me full access to all of our accounts. Part of that money needs to pay for things like the mortgage on the house, Marisa's tuition, car payments, and Jonathan's care, once I find a suitable place for him to go, but it leaves me a little bit of room to keep you on at least through the Park Manor project. After that, we can figure it out. Hopefully, by then, we'll have other clients and income rolling in so we can allocate a commensurate salary for you."

"Only if you like my work," Todd asserted.

"So far so good."

Todd grinned. "I can definitely work with that. To be honest, if I had all the money in the world, I'd work for you for free. I'm that impressed by your talent. But unfortunately, I have to pay rent, utilities, and all the other normal things of life, too."

Sabina pulled a piece of paper from her slacks pocket, sliding it across the table to Todd. "I know it's not what you deserve, but it's still in the realm of negotiable rates in this area. If you're okay with starting that way, when business builds we'll revisit the subject. I can give you enough to pay your bills, but I can't make you a millionaire."

Todd flipped over the small piece of paper and studied it for a few moments before nodding. "I can definitely work with that. Do you want me to sign a contract?"

Sabina shook her head. "I think I'm safe trusting you won't go running to the public with all my historical renovation secrets."

"On my word."

Sabina gave him a smile. "Did we have many calls yesterday?"

"Five." He got up and retrieved a notebook from the coffee table, then returned to his seat. He handed her five slips of paper. His penmanship was remarkably legible for a young guy—and he actually knew cursive, which seemed to be a dying art. "I've coded them from most to least important and told them they'd be hearing from you in a day or so."

Sabina flipped through the messages, all from guests who had attended her cocktail party. "This is terrific."

"In between calls, I made a list of the items that were nearly flushed down the toilet so you can have them replaced. I also made a list of everyone I could think of who'd hired Charles, tracked down their addresses and phone numbers, and wrote an introductory letter for you to go over. I thought we might want to send them a brochure and a business card."

Sabina grinned. "It looks like I made a very smart decision to hire you."

"You did," Todd readily agreed.

They discussed how Todd could fill his day with a myriad of tasks that needed to be completed, and while he went to work, Sabina headed for her office and returned three calls.

At eleven-thirty, Sabina's phone reminded her of her shopping date with Julie. Todd sat in the living room set with his tablet, looking at furniture samples, taking screenshots, and adding them to a file for Sabina to review for the Parkview Manor renovation.

"I need to get going. I've got a shopping date with Julie out in Greece," she said, slipping into her coat sleeves.

"Have fun."

"Not likely. I'm worried about Zoey. The closer she gets to her due date, the more anxious she is. Julie was going to see if she could get her to talk to a therapist. I'm going to kill her if she hasn't done it."

"Don't leave any DNA evidence behind. The cops always get the bad guys—and gals—because of DNA."

"I'll be especially careful," Sabina said, grabbing her purse.

Todd smiled and waved as Sabina hurried out of the showroom and to her car. Jumping inside, she texted Julie to let her know she was on her way and pulled out of the busy plaza onto Monroe Avenue.

The day was cold and bright, and it took only twenty minutes for Sabina to arrive at the mall. Parking as close to the food court as she could get, she approached the bank of plate-glass doors and saw Julie sitting at a table near the carousel, flipping through her phone, looking cross. On another day, Sabina might assume her best friend dreaded the drudgery of holiday shopping. But with everything going on in hers and Zoey's lives, Sabina suspected it more than facing the crazy crowds.

"Hello, beautiful lady," Sabina said with a smile.

Julie stood up, leaning in to hug Sabina. "Hey. I got your text but I figured I wouldn't reply since you were driving."

Sabina narrowed her eyes. "Do you want to get something to eat first, or tell me what's going on? And don't tell me nothing because I can see it in your face."

Julie took her seat once again and Sabina took the one next to her. "Zoey is driving me crazy. She's supposed to deliver in the next couple of weeks and she hasn't made a decision about the baby. I keep telling her she needs to put this baby up for adoption. And yet, part of me thinks that foster care might be an option. But then I worry about that whole system."

"Zoey voiced that same reluctance to me. She's a smart young woman."

"She's a child," Julie said. "Not just according to me, but by law, too." Julie shook her head. "I'm not a monster, but I also don't want to be a grandma and a mother to her child, because she is surely not capable of taking care of it. She doesn't understand that babies aren't stuffed animals in clothes. They're a life-long commitment, and half the time I can't even get her to put her laundry in the damn hamper."

Sabina nodded, not saying anything, just listening. It wasn't often Julie discussed the Zoey situation with her, and Sabina didn't want her to stop.

Julie shook her head. "I just wish Zoey would see how her decision affects everyone; the baby, me, and it will affect her for the rest of her life. I don't think she realizes that after the baby is born, she's not going to be able to say, 'Mom, can you watch the baby so I can go have fun?' If she lives with me, she needs to be responsible for that child twenty-four seven. She doesn't have the mental capability right now to fully grasp what it takes. I did it, and now I'm here, with just a little bit more money, still no patience, and still no life."

Sabina pursed her lips, thinking about what Julie was saying and the best way to respond to her. "I think that Zoey has a hard time understanding that even though you were married when she was born, your husband was never around. Her dad was not a father figure. You had to take care of Zoey, you were young, and you are all too aware of what that took. Honestly, I think your ex actually made things harder."

"Thank you," Julie said, with an exhaustive breath. "It's so frustrating. She thinks I'm doing this because I'm mean and not from bitter experience. I just want her to have choices in life. If she doesn't have them, her baby can end up the same way. Now it's her responsibility to make the best decisions for that little one, and the best one is not to become a fifteen-year-old mother. She's just not mature enough. And she still won't even tell me who the father is."

"Could it be because she's ashamed?"

"Of what? Who the father is? His race?"

"Not necessarily." Sabina chose her words carefully. "Perhaps that she wasn't a willing participant in this baby's conception."

The color drained from Julie's face. "That's a fancy way of saying rape."

"It's something to consider. Did you find a therapist for Zoey?"

"I called her obstetrician on Friday and she called a psychologist friend of hers and got us an emergency appointment—for *next* Monday."

Sabina gaped. "That's another whole six days."

"I know, but without her pulling strings, it might've been weeks."

Sabina reached out and took Julie's hand, giving her a half-smile. "I know things seem difficult now, but they won't always be. They *will* improve. Things tend to work out the way they're supposed to."

Julie squeezed her hand and smiled at Sabina. "Thank you." She took a deep breath. "I'm sorry to be rambling on about my problems. How're things on your side?"

Sabina flicked her brow and shrugged. "Constantly changing. The doctor at the hospital mentioned transferring Jonathan to a nursing home for long-term care. And soon. Every time my phone rings I jump, afraid it's the hospital's social worker."

Julie winced. "Yikes. A nursing home. That's gonna cost a mint."

Sabina blew out a breath. "Yeah, which is why I went to the attorney's office. Luckily, thanks to the power of attorney set up in our wills, I'm still on all the accounts. I'm the executor of the estate at this point and in charge of all of Jonathan's affairs. The only thing that's a gray area is the house. I would most likely have to go to court to evict Courtney, which doesn't sound like a pleasant experience."

"No, it doesn't. But in the end, you gotta do what you gotta do," Julie said. "And by that, I mean you do what's best for you and your daughter. Don't let your big heart get the best of you."

Sabina smiled. "I'll do my best. Right now, we're okay, and I want to see where things go with Jonathan."

They left the food court without having a bite and walked into one of the boutiques, moving along the racks browsing through the holiday dresses on offer. Of course, Sabina had no plans for the holidays at that point, and her mind was too focused on Jonathan, her showroom, and all the little bits and pieces that went along with those things. Life had become incredibly complicated, but then it always had been and Sabina tried not to let it stress her out. She wanted to be there for her friend though, and for the first time in her life, she found it hard to focus on Julie's problems when everything was so loud and in her face when it came to her own life.

They spent the rest of the day window shopping and talking about trivial things, enjoying each other's company, and picking out some simple holiday decorations for Sabina's apartment. She knew she could go over to the house and grab a few of the boxes there, but she didn't want to deal with Courtney. So, she picked out a few things and figured she would wait for Marisa to come home to do the rest.

Julie had to get back home to prepare for a client's catering event the next evening and though Sabina loved Julie to death, she was looking forward to a little bit of quiet in her tiny apartment.

She called Todd and told him she wouldn't come back to the store until the next day.

"That's okay," he assured her, sounding excited. "We had three walk-in customers who spent over a hundred bucks. Woo-hoo!"

Sabina laughed. "That's great. I'll see you tomorrow."

"I'll be here, girlfriend. See you then."

Upon arriving at her apartment, Sabina tossed her bag on the entryway table and walked into the living room. Her phone rang loudly and for a moment she considered letting it go to voice mail, but with Jonathan in the hospital and Marisa at college, she figured she should probably answer it.

Pulling her phone from her purse, Sabina accepted the Face-time call. "Hey, sweetie."

"Hey, Mom," Marisa replied. "Did I catch you at a bad time?"

Sabina laughed. "There is no good time in my life right this second but you're fine. I just got back from shopping with Julie and was about to sit down and relax."

"Oh, good," she said with an exhaustive sigh. "I was hoping I could talk to about something."

Sabina grabbed a bottle of water from the fridge and walked back into the living room, plopping down on the sofa and putting her feet up on the coffee table.

"Of course," Sabina said, steeling herself. "Hit me with it."

"Okay," Marisa said, sounding nervous. "So, I've been talking to Courtney a little bit."

Sabina lifted a brow. "What? I thought she was the devil."

Marisa's giggle sounded forced. "She is, but I'm not talking to her because I like her or anything, it's because she's pregnant with my half brother or sister. I figured I should probably keep in contact with her, especially since Dad is in the condition he's in."

Sabina took a drink of her water. "All right, and how is she doing?" Sabina asked, which was the last thing she cared about.

"Not good," Marisa said with a touch of sadness in her voice. "Obviously, she doesn't know what's going on with Dad, and she seems really stressed out. She doesn't open up that much to me, but with the baby, she seems to need to get it out of her system so I listen. Mom, Courtney has started to talk about putting the baby up for adoption."

Sabina wasn't surprised. Courtney was young, and without Jonathan by her side, she was nothing more than a paralegal. She had little status at the firm because she hadn't worked there long. In some ways, Courtney was being smart, thinking about the future in case Jonathan never recovered. Nonetheless, Sabina tried not to let it bother her, but she could tell that it concerned Marisa.

"I'm sorry about that honey," Sabina said. "How does that make you feel?"

"Horrible. I feel absolutely horrible about it," Marisa said, her voice breaking. "That's *my* brother or sister. If something bad happens to dad, that baby is the only part of him I'll have left. I don't want my sibling out there with some random family."

"I know it's hard for you to understand, sweetie, but Courtney is wise to consider what's best for the baby. He or she could go to a home where it'll be very well taken care of and loved and there's not a lot of stress. If Courtney's thinking about that then she probably doesn't think she can provide for the baby in every way possible."

"Yeah, yeah, yeah," Marisa said dismissively. "But I think I have a solution, and I just want you to hear me out."

That didn't sound encouraging.

"Okay," Sabina said cautiously.

"Since I'm now eighteen years old and technically an adult, I was thinking about telling Courtney that I would become the baby's guardian."

CHAPTER 22

*S*abina took a deep breath to stay calm. She knew that when Marisa had her heart set on something if she didn't speak calmly to her, it would escalate into a fight. Technically, Marisa was old enough to do whatever she wanted and Sabina needed to stop her from making a very big mistake.

She steadied her nerves. "Sweetheart, you truly have the biggest heart in the world, and while I admire that in you, I say this with all the love I have. I don't think you're ready to be a child's guardian."

"I know there are some speed bumps I would have to overcome," she said as though she had practiced the response in advance. "But I think that with the right guidance it could work out really well."

Sabina cleared her throat. "Marisa, I need you to really think about what doing this would entail. It's not about whether you would be a good role model for this kid, or if you would love it, it's about all the other things in life,"

"Mom," Marisa wailed.

"You're a college student," Sabina continued, "and a brand-new one at that. You have no other means of support, other than me and your father."

"I know that, but it's not like Dad wouldn't take care of his own kid. He may not be physically able to do that right now, but next year he could be perfectly fine," Marisa said, frustration edging into her voice.

"He could be," Sabina replied. "I'm not trying to rain on your parade, but until your father gets better, if he does, I'm the one who has to take care of everything financially. I will be the person who is supporting everyone and that includes Miss Courtney who's living in our house while I pay the mortgage. That includes all of the care for your father, which is going to be mega expensive, and everything you need. On top of that, I have a new business and myself to take care of, as well."

"You just don't want to take care of this baby because it's Courtney's," Marisa said angrily.

Sabina lifted both eyebrows and contemplated what she was about to say, figuring she might as well be blunt so the conversation didn't keep going around and around. "You're right. I know it's not the baby's fault, but there is no way that I'm going to be responsible for my ex-husband's love child. Now that you're in college, and your father left me for another woman, I created my own career, one that I've wanted my whole life but had to put on hold for you and your father. With all that in mind, don't you think it's more than a little unfair to ask me to take on that kind of responsibility?"

Marisa was quiet for several moments and to Sabina's surprise, when she finally did respond, she sounded more defeated than angry. "I know it sounds insane. I know it's a crazy idea and it's not right for me to ask you. I'm just trying to keep my brother or sister in my life, and I'm afraid that Courtney's just going to hand the baby off to the first person who'll take it."

Sabina's heart went out to her daughter. "Honey, I know, but what you can do is make sure to continuously keep in touch with

Courtney, and maybe there'll be a way that she can connect you with whoever will be adopting the baby. A lot of adoptive parents are allowing open adoptions where the birth family stays in the baby's life. Honestly, though, this is all very early in the game to even be thinking about it. For all we know your father could be back on his feet next week and everything will go back to just the way it was. Courtney won't give that baby away if your father is better. And nothing will happen until the baby's born in a couple of months."

Marisa groaned. "I guess you're right. I can only hope that Dad gets better soon. I was really hoping he would be better by the time I came back for Christmas, but when I called the nurses to check in on him, they said he was the same as the last time I was there. But anyway, I figured it was worth talking to you about."

"I'm sorry I can't be more supportive."

"Yeah, well. I guess I understand. Look, I've got to get going. I have to study for a quiz tomorrow."

"Good luck, sweetie," Sabina replied. "I can't wait until you come back home."

"Thanks, Mom. See ya."

Sabina tapped the end-call icon, set her phone aside, and let her head fall back against the couch, closing her eyes. That went better than she expected. There'd been times when Marisa could barely get through a day without throwing a fit. How she thought she could take care of a baby, Sabina had no idea. Oddly enough, through all of the turmoil and trouble with Julie, Sabina had always sided with Zoey. She felt it was Zoey's choice to keep her baby, regardless of her age. But after listening to Marisa, Sabina found herself firmly in Julie's court. No way in hell did she want to bring up the child of the woman who broke up her marriage.

Sabina's phone pinged. She grabbed it and saw the text was from Steve, giving her a much-needed smile.

Hey there beautiful, Just wanted to check in. What's up?

She texted him back.

The normal stuff. Shopping with my neurotic best friend, taking care of my ex-husband, trying to figure out how to get my ex-husband's girlfriend who's pregnant with his baby to move out of my house, oh, and my daughter has decided she wants to adopt her little brother or sister. Just the usual.

It took a second longer than normal for Steve to text her back and she knew it was because he must have been staring at the message in disbelief.

Finally, the phone pinged again.

Wow. That's a lot of stuff going on at one time, and none of it sounds very fun.

Sabina let out a breath, wishing she could hang out with Steve. She hadn't spoken to him since Thanksgiving, and even then cooking and football had been tops on the agenda. It seemed like something was *always* going on to keep them apart. Whether it was Marisa's breakdown over her father, having to take care of Jonathan, or her business, making plans with the guy she hoped to eventually date had become challenging.

Yeah, it's no fun at all. But such is life. I'm sorry that I haven't reached out to you. Honestly, it's not that you haven't been on my mind.

Steve replied.

It's perfectly fine. To be honest, if I was going through what you are, I'm not sure anybody would want to see my face.

Sabina rubbed the bridge of her nose.

There've been several times that I thought about calling and just seeing if you wanted to go get food or play in traffic, but every single time, without fail, somebody knocks on my door, she texted.

Just as she finished the sentence, pounding on her front door rang out across her tiny apartment.

She tilted her head to one side and staring at the door.

See? Jesus, it never fails.

Steve replied. *What? Is someone at your door?*

The knock rang out again and Sabina groaned, pulling her tired body off the couch. Sending him a quick text.

Yep. It never fails.

She walked over to the door, glanced through the peephole, and opened it up, letting Todd in before turning and shuffling back over to the couch. Todd made his way inside carrying two bags and the Parkview Manor renovation binder. She wasn't even sure how she could get her brain to start working, let alone come up with fantastic ideas to make the place tour-worthy again.

Sabina glanced at her phone to see Steve's latest text. *Listen, I won't keep you but I just wanted you to know I was thinking about you. Next time you have a minute of peace and quiet, even if it's only five minutes, call and feel free to unload.*

Sabina smiled and tapped a quick message back.

Thanks. And don't feel like you can't call. My phone is on me at all times these days and I'll always answer your call if I can. I promise we'll get together soon and pick up wherever it was that we left off.

Steve replied right away.

Sounds good to me, and I'm not going anywhere, either. This will pass and things will start to settle down again.

I hope so.

Sabina stood there staring at the blank screen for several moments feeling lucky to have met someone like Steve. Still, she knew he wouldn't wait forever, but she hoped events in her life would calm down enough that she could at least have dinner with him again before he ran off into the sunset. He was the first guy Sabina had feelings for since meeting Jonathan and he'd shown by example that he was a really good guy.

Todd took off his jacket, setting it on one of the peninsula's stools, and cleared his throat.

"I thought we were done working for the day," Sabina said and set her phone on the counter.

"I brought all this stuff over so you could go through it

tonight. We have a meeting with Georgia Wilcox tomorrow morning to discuss the Parkview Manor renovations. I figured it would be more efficient for us to meet there."

Sabina scowled, eyeing the bags filled with fabric and other samples. "I almost forgot about that. I don't know what I'd do without you."

Smiling, Todd put the bags and binder down and leaned against the kitchen's peninsula. "You can go even crazier than you're already doing."

Sabina squinted at him. "I'd fight with you, but what's the point?"

Needing a caffeine jolt, she dragged herself into the kitchen, filled the reservoir, added a filter and ground beans, and turned on the coffeemaker. She knew she wouldn't be able to fall asleep later, but she felt exhausted now. Todd's phone went off and he pulled it out of his pocket, a big grin lighting up his face.

"Who's that?"

Todd cleared his throat. "It's your daughter. She's trying to figure out what to wear for the holidays and sent me a picture of herself in a reindeer sweater and a pair of snowman leggings."

Sabina smiled as she grabbed a cup, periodically glancing at Todd as he typed away on his keypad. Her smile faded, however as she studied his facial expressions. She remembered everything Julie had said about him on Thanksgiving. The way Todd's cheeks blushed, the excitement in his eyes, the funny little chuckle—everything a man did when talking to a beautiful woman. Todd didn't look like a friendly gay man chatting with a friend; he looked like a schoolboy in love. Sabina knew that look all too well.

She poured herself a cup of coffee and leaned against the counter, taking a sip. She waited until he stopped texting to speak. "By the way, I forgot to tell you. I met the most amazing guy the other day. He's handsome, rich, fashionable, and gay. I told him that I had a single friend and I figured maybe the two of you could get together for dinner or something. Maybe we could make it a double date with Steve."

She took another sip of coffee, watching as his body suddenly tensed.

"Uh..." He cleared his throat several times. "Wonderful as that sounds, I'm...uh...not really on the market right now. Thanks though."

Sabina slowly lowered her cup and scowled. Todd gave her a double look. "What?"

She clicked her tongue and shook her head. "I knew it. Well, Julie knew it and I think deep down I knew it, too."

Todd narrowed his eyes. "What are you talking about?"

She sat her coffee cup down and advanced on him until she was right in his face. "Just admit it, you're not gay. In fact, not only are you *not* gay but you have a crush on my daughter."

Todd scoffed. "You're being ridiculous. I am Mister freaking rainbow sparkles himself."

Sabina pursed her lips and crossed her arms, staring straight at him. Todd squirmed under her gaze, but after a few moments of her giving him her best mom stare, his shoulders slumped and it seemed as though he lost a couple of inches of height.

"Okay, fine. No, I'm not actually gay."

Sabina scowled once again. "Why did you tell me that, then?"

Todd rolled his eyes and turned toward her, putting his phone down on the counter. "It was easier than being a macho guy who's into interior design. I tried that for two years and nobody wanted to hire me. When I walked into a place and stunk it up with my heterosexuality, everyone turned their heads. As soon as I pretended I was gay, suddenly the job offers came flooding in and clients wanted to work with me. It was an accident at first really, with the knowledge I have of interior design, people automatically thought I *was* gay, and I just never corrected them. It turned into a thing though, and I've been pretty much living a double life. I won't lie, it's been freaking exhausting."

Sabina contemplated the range of outrage she could throw him, but the truth was she wasn't really angry. Everything he said made perfect sense. She had been in the interior design business long enough to know that you were either a busybody, a home-maker, a high-end decorator, or a gay man. She was pretty sure she had never met a straight male interior designer before. There was a reason for stereotypes, after all.

Todd's phone pinged again and Sabina eyed it on the counter. "And Marisa?"

Todd shrugged his shoulders. "I guess in a way yeah, I do have feelings for her. She's amazing. I mean I don't have to tell you that."

"Who also happens to be seven years younger than you and barely an adult. And I mean adult as in legally she's an adult, but emotionally she's more like fifteen years old." Sabina picked up her coffee again and waited for him to reply.

"I know you're right," he admitted, "but feelings are feelings. It's not like you can just turn them off."

Sabina took a step back and tried to come up with the right reply. "Don't take this the wrong way because it's not personal. Obviously, I like you, but you're too old for my daughter, and on top of that *she* thinks you're gay. That's a recipe for disaster and I have enough disasters in my life right now. But I'll tell you this; if you plan on pursuing Marisa, you can't go on working for me. It would get far too complicated and messy."

Todd pouted and shuffled his feet. "I guess I can understand that." He sighed. "I'll keep my feelings to myself and carry on as usual. Besides, I think Marisa needs a friend more than anything else at this point."

Sabina reached out and squeezed his shoulder. "Thanks. If we can get going on the Parkview Manor renovation, and then work on obtaining the clients Charles swindled, you might just have a permanent position with Sabina Reigns Designs."

"Excellent." But then he blushed. "Uh, I'm not usually one to celebrate someone else's failure, but Charles deserves it."

Sabina nodded. "Since we're tackling tough conversations, why don't you enlighten me as to why you left him in the first place."

Todd groaned. "Do I have to?"

Sabina shrugged. "Well no, I can't force you, but I bet you'd feel better if you got it off your chest."

Todd took in a deep breath and nodded. "Well, now that you know I'm not gay, this will make even more sense to you. As you well know, he never really did any of his own designs. One night, when all of his female proteges were out and about spending his money, he came into the room where I was drawing and made a pass at *me*. I told him that I wasn't interested, then he back-tracked and basically told me that I was too full of myself to think he'd want me. After three years working for that skinflint, I'd had it—and I let him know it. He started calling me an ingrate, made a lot of homophobic slurs, and then fired me."

Sabina shook her head. "I'm sorry you had to go through that. Even if you were gay, I would slap you around if you had said yes to that fool. He's probably not feeling too self-important these days though."

Todd offered a half-hearted grin and reached over to grab his jacket. "I guess I should get out of here. We have an important meeting tomorrow morning at Parkview Manor."

Sabina's phone rang, and Todd glanced down, reading out the name on the screen.

"It's Julie."

Sabina had her hands in the sink rinsing out her coffee cup. "Could you answer that for me real quick?"

Todd put the phone to his ear. "Sabina's phone. How can I help you?"

Sabina grinned and shook her head as she dried off her hands. She wasn't going to give away Todd's secret. He hadn't spoken since he first greeted Julie. Slowly, Sabina turned to see Todd standing there with his hand over his mouth, and the phone pressed to his ear. His concerned gaze shifted up toward Sabina and a shiver ran up her back.

Hurrying over, she took the phone from Todd. "What's wrong, Julie?"

Julie's voice cracked. "I'm standing in the emergency room waiting for Zoey to get back from having an ultrasound. I rushed her to the ER."

"What happened?" Sabina asked,

"When I came home, I found Zoey lying on the couch. She said she'd had the cramps all afternoon. She thought it was from the tacos she had for lunch at school. But then she casually mentioned that she hadn't felt the baby move in a couple of days and wondered if she should be worried." Julie let out a shaky breath. "Apparently nobody told her it was important to pay attention to that and when we got here, they couldn't find a fetal heartbeat."

"Oh dear God."

"This is my punishment," Julie said with deadly calm. "God is punishing me because I didn't want to welcome that baby into our home."

"Don't you dare say that," Sabina warned and headed for the entryway to grab her coat and purse. "It's rush hour, but I'll be there as soon as I can."

"Thank you," Julie said, her voice breaking.

"Love you," Sabina assured her friend and stabbed the call-end icon. She looked over at Todd who put his hand out. "I'll drive. I can get us there faster."

They hurried out the door and headed for Todd's Prius, Sabina's mind awhirl, grateful Todd had been there. Her hands were shaking and she was so frightened she wasn't sure she was capable of driving across the city to get back to Greece. After everything Zoey and Julie had been through, it seemed cruel to taunt them with this situation.

They got in the car and Todd started the engine. The radio came on with Burl Ives belting out "Rudolph The Red-Nosed Reindeer." Todd punched the off button, shoved the car into gear, and pulled out of the parking space.

CHAPTER 23

Sabina stood at the window, watching the rain pour down outside. She traced the raindrops with her fingers, looking through the rivulets at the distorted images in the distance. She found it remarkable how inside one room the entire world could stop, while on the outside, everything kept moving. Life was funny that way. You could be going through something devastating, and nearby someone else might be experiencing the greatest joy of their life.

Zoey was experiencing devastation. So was her Mom.

Sabina glanced at her watch. It was almost eleven. She'd been at the hospital for almost six hours, waiting. Todd had been game to stay with her in the waiting area in the birthing center, but she'd sent him home several hours earlier. "But how will you get home?"

She shrugged. "Uber."

"Okay." He'd left her, only to reappear half an hour later with some sandwiches, chips, and a cup of Starbuck's best brew.

"You didn't need to do that."

"Hey, I gotta keep you on your feet, boss," he said, handing off the bag. "I got something for Julie, too."

"I'm not sure she'll be hungry, but thanks."

"What do you want to do about the meeting tomorrow morning?" Todd asked.

Sabina had sighed. "I don't know. I'll let you know."

He nodded. "Do you need a hug or anything?"

Sabina offered a wan smile. "You are a mind reader." She fell into his tender embrace.

When Julie appeared half an hour later, Sabina offered her the sandwich. "Thanks, but I don't think I can eat. I'm just too wired."

"How's Zoey?"

Julie sighed. "Not well. She's pretty upset."

"What happened?" Sabina asked as they hadn't had a real chance to talk.

Julie's shoulders sagged. "Her water must have broken overnight. She thought she wet the bed and was afraid to tell me. So she tossed her sheets in the washing machine, ate a breakfast burrito, and went off to school as usual."

"What about the contractions?" Sabina asked.

Julie shrugged. "Zoey hadn't realized the cramps she felt were labor pains. She told me it just felt like having a bad period."

"Didn't her doctor prepare her for this?"

"I didn't go in with her every time. I'm ashamed to say I was too angry. But I'm sure they warned her, but I think she was in denial this morning, hoping the cramps would just go away. She wasn't due for another couple of weeks." Julie's eyes filled with tears. "I feel awful about making her go to school until the last minute. I figured as I had to keep working until the contractions started with her, she should have to go to school. God, what a fucking awful mother I am."

"Oh, Jules, don't be so hard on yourself."

"You say that now, but I know that's not how you feel. Every time I complained about Zoey getting knocked up, I could see it in your eyes. You stood by me because we're best friends, but you were disappointed in me—and I was so damned stubborn…" Her voice cracked and she began to sob.

Sabina wrapped her arms around her friend, patting her back. When Julie pulled back, Sabina fished a clean tissue from her pocket, pressing it into Julie's hand.

"How the labor going?"

"She's at ten centimeters. I hope it won't be long—for Zoey's sake and mine," she ruefully admitted. "They're giving her pain meds, but the faster she delivers the better it'll be for both of us."

Me, too, Sabina thought. She had that meeting with Georgia Wilcox about the Parkview Manor renovation at nine the next morning. And yet, there was no way she could abandon Julie and Zoey—no matter how important that meeting was to her business. She'd just have to send Todd and hope he could do a half-decent presentation. And then she remembered that he'd brought all the materials to her apartment. God, what a hot mess. She'd have to call or text him early in the morning to have him try to reschedule the meeting.

Julie spoke again. "I'd better get back to Zoey."

"Yes, of course. Send her my love."

"I will."

Sabina sat down again and took out the small notebook she kept in her purse. She liked to make lists; they kept her focused. She could write them on her phone, but she preferred to put them down on paper. Sometimes the old-fashioned ways worked best.

Four lists and several hours later, Julie returned to the waiting room.

"It's over," she said her voice shaky. "Zoey just delivered the placenta. They took the baby away, but the nurse will be coming in to ask if Zoey wants to see it."

"Her," Sabina reminded her.

"Yeah," Julie said. "Zoey wants you to come back to the room.

They said to give them a few minutes to clean her up. "Do you want to go in?"

Sabina took an uncertain breath. No! She didn't want to go in. She wanted to creep away and not face Zoey, not knowing what to say or how to offer comfort. "Of course," she said and forced a smile. She grabbed her purse and the still-uneaten sandwich and followed Julie through the double doors.

The head of the bed was cranked high and Zoey rested against it looking pale and exhausted. Sabina rushed forward and hugged her. "Hello, sweetie."

"Hey," Zoey said, her voice a whisper.

Sabina pulled back. "Are you hungry?" What a stupid thing to say, but she carried on. "Todd brought a sandwich for your Mom, but she didn't want it."

Zoey shook her head.

Before Sabina could blurt anything else embarrassing, one of the nurses returned.

"Zoey, would you like to hold your daughter?"

Zoey looked to her mother, panicked.

Julie sat down next to Zoey and held her hand.

Sabina retreated to the window, letting them have their moment.

"This is your choice, honey. No one will look down on you if you say no, but if you say yes, I'll be right here with you. It'll be one of the hardest things you will ever do, but it will only make you stronger."

Sabina shot a look over her shoulder. After the grueling process of childbirth, Zoey looked so damn fragile. But one thing she did not resemble was a young girl. Not anymore. She held up her chin with that same strength her mother possessed and nodded at the nurse.

"I want to prepare you for what you'll see."

"Prepare?" Zoey asked.

"Yes, your baby's skin will look…dark. Like she's bruised."

"I don't understand," Zoey said.

"It's called maceration."

"Isn't that like when your fingers get pruney after being soaked in water?" Julie asked.

The nurse nodded.

Julie turned back to her daughter. "You don't have to do this," she reminded Zoey.

"Yeah, Mom, I do."

The nurse gave her a sad smile and turned and left the room.

"I'm scared," Zoey whispered, just loud enough for Sabina to hear.

"It'll be okay," Julie said softly and kissed to top of her daughter's head.

A minute later, the nurse returned with a tiny bundle. The baby was swaddled in a pink receiving blanket and a matching knitted cap, Zoey took a deep breath, her eyes growing watery and held out her arms. Sabina watched Zoey become the mother that Julie hadn't had the faith she could be. Sabina watched as Zoey cradled the dusky-skinned baby, kiss her sweet little face, and hold her to her breast.

"Hello, Robin," Zoey whispered. "I'm sorry...I'm so, so sorry. I..." But then she couldn't continue and closed her eyes, tenderly holding onto her dead child. Silent tears ran down her cheeks. Julie's eyes filled as she dabbed a tissue near the corners of Zoey's eyes, whispering words Sabina couldn't hear. But they weren't intended for her, and that was okay.

Zoey looked up, her lips trembling. "Aunt Sabina, will you take some pictures of us?"

Sabina swallowed and found it hard to speak. "Sure, sweetie." She took out her phone and snapped picture after picture of both Zoey and Julie holding the baby, realizing how precious those photos would be to them in the future.

After rocking her baby for what seemed like forever, but could only have been twenty or so minutes, Zoey asked her mother to hand her little girl back to the nurse. Sabina could see the devastation in Julie's eyes. Her breath was heavy as she struggled to keep the tears at bay. Julie hugged the baby tightly and stood up from the bed, walking toward the room's door which stood ajar. And then Zoey began to cry in earnest, finally giving in to the sorrow that ravaged her heart.

Sabina clasped her hand over her mouth, tears streaming down her cheeks as she watched her best friend stand with her back to her daughter, her shoulders gently shaking from her own release of emotion. A nurse appeared and took the baby from Julie and closed the door. Somehow, Julie managed to collect herself, wiped her tears, and turned back to her daughter. Then she crawled in alongside Zoey and cradled her in her arms, just as she had done fifteen years before when she'd given birth to her. It was sad, so incredibly sad, but at the same time beautiful.

Julie held her daughter in her arms until Zoey finally cried herself to sleep.

A few minutes later, a woman poked her head inside the door. "Mrs. Baxter?"

Gently, Julie extricated herself from her sleeping child and joined her at the door. Sabina crept forward, trying not to intrude, but wanting to be there in case Julie needed her.

"Could we talk in private," the woman began, throwing a glance over Julie's shoulder to take in Sabina.

"This is my dearest friend. You can say anything in front of her."

The woman nodded and motioned them into the hall. They followed.

"If you're up to it," the woman began, "we need to talk about what happens next."

"Next?" Julie said. She didn't seem to understand.

"Would you prefer burial or cremation? And would you like to authorize an autopsy?"

Sabina's breath caught in her throat. She held back from

hugging Julie because she could tell her friend was holding on by a thread, a thread that needed to stay intact just a little while longer.

"I—I..." Julie began.

"Why don't you go and talk with..." Sabina didn't know what the woman's title was. Social worker? Grief counselor? Bean-counter in general.

Julie just stared at Sabina for long seconds.

"I'll stay with Zoey."

Julie nodded dumbly and when the woman turned, she started after her—a step behind.

Sabina reentered Zoey's room and found the silence unnerving. She tiptoed close to the bed and sat down in the lone chair, watching Zoey for several minutes before restlessness captured her and she turned to the window, pulling the drape back just enough to see that the rain had turned to snow.

It hadn't occurred to Sabina that Jonathan was in a hospital across the city. She hadn't visited him or even kept her promise to Marisa to call every day. She hadn't heard from the staff about moving him to a nursing home for rehab, either. She thought about Marisa making plans to come back home for the holidays, and she thought about Courtney, sitting in Sabina's old house, surrounded by someone else's life, a child growing inside of her, and a fear that was growing even faster. Courtney wasn't thinking about saying hello to her baby—and probably not even goodbye. Jonathan's love child had now become a big problem for its mother.

Sabina's thoughts were interrupted by the sound of Zoey in the bed behind her, situating herself. She winced as she pulled her body upward on the pillows, no longer asleep. Sabina raced to her side. "Careful honey. You're going to be very sore for quite a while. I can get the nurse and see if you can have some more pain medication."

Zoey nodded but then changed her mind. "Maybe in a

minute. I've been drugged up since I got here, and I just want to feel everything for a moment. Everything has been so cloudy."

Sabina nodded, sitting on the edge of the bed as close to Zoey as she could, hoping to make her feel safe and secure. Sabina had been a presence in Zoey's life since the day she was born, but they had never been particularly close. It was more like an aunt and niece type of relationship. But in those moments, she could tell that Zoey felt comfortable, or maybe it was just that she needed to talk.

"Where's Mom?"

"Uh…she's speaking to some of the people on staff about…" But then she couldn't say the words.

Zoey seemed to understand and nodded silently.

"I never got to tell my mother what I decided," Zoey said, staring toward the window. "I kept it from her because I didn't want to fight with her anymore. She thinks I didn't understand what she was trying to say. She thinks that I'm naïve about how hard it would be to raise a child at my age. But I'm not. I knew that I'd have to give up everything I ever wanted because my baby would be the most important thing to me. And though I thought about everything Mom told me, even if I didn't say it, I knew from the beginning what I was going to do—even if Mom kicked us out."

Sabina reached out and took Zoey's hand as tears began to stream down her face again. Zoey took a deep breath, wiping the tears away angrily. "I was going to keep Robin. How could I not? She was just a little soul. How could I hand her to someone that she never knew? But Mom wasn't about to let me make that choice. That choice was ripped away from me."

"I don't think so. Your Mom ranted and raved, but she loves you with all her heart, and she would have fallen in love with Robin the minute she saw her."

"You don't know that."

"Oh, but I do. Your Mom's been my best friend since we were

in third grade. I know her heart and soul, and I know her bluff and bluster, too."

"Really?" Zoey asked, tears filling her eyes once more.

"You bet. And though Robin won't be a part of your lives going forward, you had some of the most precious time with her —a time when you didn't have to share her with anyone. Where she felt the most secure and safe that she ever would because you were holding her inside of you and allowing her to grow."

Zoey glanced at Sabina, her face softening a bit. She gave a small nod and wiped her tears again, sniffling. Sabina reached over and grabbed a tissue. Zoey wiped her nose and shook her head. "I'm really angry. And I know no matter how many times my mother tried to change my mind, and how many times she refused to think about keeping Robin, I guess I know she's hurting too. I want to yell at her, I want to tell her how horrible she's been, but she's all I have right now. And since we came to the hospital, she hasn't said a negative word or made an angry face at me. When it really mattered she was with me, holding my hand. I'm trying really hard not to show that anger."

Sabina smiled. "I know you think you're completely different than her, but you're not. You have the biggest heart. Sitting here in one of your darkest moments, you're still capable of thinking about someone else. And you're capable of beginning to forgive someone who hurt you very deeply. I'm so proud of you for that, Zoey. I wish I could give you a reason for why these things happen, but I can tell you that it's made you become a different person. And you'll never stop loving or forget Robin. She'll always have a place in your heart."

Zoey looked at Sabina with her big doe eyes and squeezed her hand. "My daughter didn't have the chance to take a breath, but she taught me a lot. How powerful is that?"

Sabina's breath caught in her throat, caught off guard by how mature Zoey had suddenly become.

"I know this is a sore subject," Sabina began, "but will you tell Robin's father what happened?"

Zoey's head snapped up, her eyes blazing. "No!"

"Is it because of the way Robin was conceived."

"What does that mean?"

Sabina chose her words carefully. "That you weren't a willing participant in her conception."

Zoey looked startled. "You're asking if I was raped?"

"Is that what happened?"

"No. No!" Zoey repeated, sounding shocked. "We were just fooling around...and then...it happened. We only did it the one time. It was an accident."

"Did you ever tell this boy that you were pregnant?"

"Everybody at school knew," Zoey muttered, her gaze sinking.

"Then...?"

"It's none of your business," Zoey began, but then another tear cascaded down her cheek. She wiped it away.

"I'm sorry," Sabina whispered.

Zoey shrugged. "I guess it doesn't matter anymore."

Sabina waited.

Finally, Zoey sighed. "His family didn't need any more grief."

"What does that mean."

"Taylor's father was killed by a drunk driver back when the school year started. There's five kids in that family. His mom had to get a second job."

"That's terrible, but—"

Zoey shook her head. She looked like she wanted to say more, but before she could respond, the door opened and her mother came back into the room. The nurse was trailing behind her with a syringe.

Julie stepped up to the other side of the bed and kissed Zoey on the forehead. "The nurse is here to give you more pain medication if you need it."

Zoey nodded. "I just want to sleep."

Julie and Sabina moved away as the nurse injected the meds into the IV. Zoey closed her eyes and pulled the covers up to her chin, closing her eyes. The nurse gestured toward the door and they preceded her out. Once in the hall, the nurse spoke. "Why don't you two take a walk, maybe get some fresh air or something to eat. Zoey will need you to be strong for her when you come back."

"Thanks," Julie said. She sounded as exhausted as her daughter.

The nurse turned away and Sabina tucked her arm around Julie's and led her down the hall in silence giving her friend a chance to breathe, not having to speak, not having to feel.

Julie let Sabina lead her away from the birthing center and hung a right at the chapel.

"I didn't think you were very religious."

"I'm not, but there's rarely anyone here, and the bathroom tucked away nearby isn't used much."

"How did you find out about this?"

"I spent a lot of time here after my father had a stroke." Sabina walked Julie over to one of the pews and they sat next to each other.

Julie stared at the ground for several moments before looking over at Sabina. "I was so angry at Zoey. For the last five months, I wished that the baby would not be a part of our lives, that Zoey would wise up and not ruin everything for herself and that child. And that's exactly what happened."

Julie took in a deep breath and tilted her head back, closing her eyes. "This is never how I meant it to be. I was so stubborn and I should've just listened to Zoey. For all I know, the stress and anger that I bombarded her with played a part in what happened here today." Julie opened her eyes and stared at the ceiling.

Sabina shook her head. "You can't put this on yourself, Julie. Even Zoey knows you didn't cause this."

Julie sat up straighter. "Yes, but—"

"Robin may have looked perfect, but something went terribly wrong. Did you arrange for an autopsy?"

"Much as I hate the thought of it, yes. I don't think Zoey can get past this if she doesn't know what happened. When she has another baby—she'd be terrified to think the same thing will happen again.

"And what about afterward?" Sabina asked.

"In the morning, we'll talk about arrangements for Robin. I don't like the idea of burying her in the cold ground. If Zoey prefers to scatter her ashes when the warm weather comes, we'll figure out something appropriate."

Sabina nodded.

"What did you guys talk about while I was gone?" Julie asked.

Zoey hadn't sworn her to secrecy, but Sabina wondered if she should mention Taylor. Months before, Julie had joked about murdering the one responsible for Zoey's pregnancy—and Sabina had played along, but now....

"She told me why she didn't want to reveal Robin's father's name."

Julie perked right up. "And?" she demanded.

"It seems the boy's father died suddenly back in September. She didn't want to cause the family any more pain."

"But it was okay for her to cause me pain?" Julie remarked, sounding hurt.

"Jules," Sabina admonished.

Julie covered her eyes with a hand. "I'm sorry. I can barely think." She shook her head. "Of course she'd try spare that family pain."

"It's never wrong to show some compassion."

"And apparently more than I'm capable of," Julie muttered and sighed, slouching back against the pew. She leaned her head on Sabina's shoulder. "Thank you for being my friend—even when I'm a terrible bitch."

"You've been through thick and thin with me, too, girl," Sabina whispered, putting her arm around Julie's shoulder.

They sat on the bench for almost an hour, not saying much, just thinking. And when their backsides began to ache from sitting on the hard pew, they went in search of something to eat before heading back to Zoey's room.

"I'm going to stay the night," Julie said before entering.

"I'll be right here with you."

"You will not. I know you've got that big meeting in the morning."

Sabina looked at her watch. It was after two. "I told Todd to go home. I'm stuck here."

"Call for an Uber. I'll pay for it."

"You will not."

"Go home," Julie said, then gave Sabina a hug.

"Okay. But if you need me."

"I've got you on speed-dial," Julie said and somehow managed a wan smile.

They tip-toed into Zoey's room where Sabina retrieved her coat and purse. "Call me," she mouthed.

Julie nodded and hugged her, holding on for a long moment, and then pulled away and Sabina stole from the room.

Sabina left the birthing center and walked the long corridor toward the emergency room's waiting from. Before entering, she took out her phone and called for a ride. "Twenty minutes," she was assured and hung up.

Once again, Sabina stood at the window, watching big fluffy snowflakes fall to the ground. She traced the melted rivulets on the glass with her fingers, looking at the distorted lights from the houses across from the hospital and the lone cars that passed now and then.

For the first time in months, she was glad to be going back to the crummy little apartment across town.

She was glad she was going home.

CHAPTER 24

"*P*ersonally, I like the rugs that are new but look vintage," Miss Wilcox said, as she looked through some of the catalogs that Sabina had brought to the Parkview Manor. She felt like death on toast, but she'd dressed in her most conservative suit, slapped on some make-up so it didn't look like she'd only received three hours sleep, and made it to Parkview Manor right on time, albeit an hour later than originally planned. Todd had already arrived and was waiting for her.

"Ready or not, here we go," he said and sported a hopeful grin.

"Think about how much foot traffic this home will see once it's open to the public once again," Miss Wilcox continued. "If we put vintage rugs in here that are as old as this home, they'll be destroyed in no time, which is just a waste. Synthetic fibers will last longer and stand up to the wear and tear just a bit better."

Sabina glanced at Todd who was taking notes while Miss Wilcox spoke. "I completely agree with you. Not to mention the fact that the recreations are about a third the cost. That will leave a lot more money for the other things that you might want to do to restore this beautiful old home."

Miss Wilcox smiled. "Perfect. I appreciate your thinking that way. The benefactors paying for this restoration will appreciate a bit of financial restraint. That was not something that I saw would be an option with Mr. Patterson."

Sabina glanced over at Todd who ducked his head, struggling to hold back a smirk. Sabina picked up the various samples and packed them away.

"Well, I think we have everything we need to get started on the design. I should have mockups for you next week, including all of the things you've chosen within the next three weeks. If you have any questions or you want to change anything, just give me a call. Or if I'm not available, speak to my assistant and he'll give all your suggestions to me."

"Very well."

Sabina stood. "And thank you so much for allowing us to meet a bit later this morning."

"Well, after Mr. Foreman told me about the death in your family, it was the least I could do."

Sabina nodded and Miss Wilcox saw them out of the manor. They walked to the parking lot at the side of the home.

"So how's Zoey?" Todd asked.

"Devastated. I'll tell you all about it later."

Todd nodded. "Are you sure you don't want me to go to the hospital with you?" Todd asked.

Sabina shook her head. "No, I'll be fine. I'll see Jonathan's social worker and probably fill out some paperwork. Then I'll check in on Jonathan's progress and let Marisa know how he's doing. I'll call or text you to let you know when I'll be back at the shop."

Todd nodded. "All right, if you need me, I'll be around. But first, I'll hit the craft store to get some foam core so that when you're ready to start the mockups, we'll have everything we need."

Sabina gave him a stout nod. "Oh, and also, if you want to start reaching out to some of the old clients that Charles

Patterson left hanging and those from the grand opening, feel free. But don't schedule anything until after the first of the year. We have enough going on between now and then."

Todd grinned. "You got it."

Sabina climbed in her car and adjusted her mirrors before taking a deep breath and turning the key. Just before she was about to leave for the Manor, she'd received a call that morning saying that Jonathan was awake and that he'd made some progress during the previous few days. He wasn't speaking or fully understanding everything the doctor said to him, but awake was better than unconscious. It was time to discuss moving him to a long-term care facility.

During the drive, Sabina decided to call Julie once she got to the hospital. She figured Zoey would probably be released that day—if she hadn't already gone home. It seemed a crime that insurance companies shoved patients out the door whether they were ready or not. Sabina knew that Zoey would be very glad to get home and relax a little bit. Zoey hadn't decided whether she wanted to have an actual service or not. She felt as though the emotions about it would be mixed and might stir feelings of anger within her that she wasn't able to deal with.

Pulling up to the hospital, Sabina parked in the multi-level garage, then made her way to the social worker's office.

"Mrs. Miller—it's good to meet you," said the young woman who stood when Sabina knocked on her office door. "I'm Cheryl Dawson."

Sabina shook her hand. The woman looked young—really young. Like she had graduated from college the week before. But she must have been on the job for a while because the desk in her tiny office was heaped with file folders. There was just enough room for a file cabinet and one visitors' chair.

"As you know," Cheryl began, "your husband has made enough improvement that we think he's ready to start the rehab he'll need to return to a useful life."

Useful life? What did that mean? The social worker probably wasn't qualified to make that assessment. Her job was to get the patient out of the hospital and ship him off to someone else's care.

"Now, there's a bed open in Penfield and several in Utica."

"Utica?" Sabina blurted. "But that's a three-hour drive down the Thruway!"

Cheryl's expression was somber. "There are a lot of sick and elderly people in the county. There are two ways a bed can open up. If someone actually recovers enough to go home or, unfortunately, if someone dies. Now, I can give you half an hour to think about it, and then—"

Was she serious? Ship Jonathan off to a city he'd never been to, where it would hard for Marisa to visit?

Cheryl awaited an answer.

"We'll take the Penfield bed," Sabina said flatly.

"Excellent. I'll get the paperwork going and we can have Mr. Miller transferred sometime tomorrow. There will be a charge for the medical transport vehicle, of course."

"Of course." Money grew on trees—hang the cost!

Cheryl stood, a pretty obvious dismissal. "We'll be in touch."

Sabina bit her tongue so as not to make a snide remark.

With that out of the way, she made her way to the floor above and Jonathan's room. She didn't like that floor. Despite the hustle and bustle of nurses, techs, and workers pushing food carts, she hated walking the gauntlet of sick and elderly people slumped in wheelchairs that cluttered the halls. She supposed it got them out of their bleak rooms, but seeing those old, sweet faces vacant-eyed, not reacting, just existing, and often with no visitors to break up their long, lonely days, was heartbreaking.

Of course, she'd left Jonathan on his own for days on end and was as guilty as those families that seemed to have abandoned their elderly. Several times since Jonathan had arrived she'd seen family members in tears, holding each other. It made her feel depressed every time she visited.

But Jonathan was different. He was half the age of most of the floor's stroke victims. And as his fiancé, it was Courtney who should have been there holding his hand. That she'd apparently abandoned him after less than two weeks said a lot about her character. Would she have done the same after she'd taken a vow to love and honor him through sickness and in health?

Squelching the flare of anger that coursed through her, Sabina checked in at the nurses' station, which was attended to by personnel she hadn't met before.

"Hello. I'm Mrs. Miller here to see my—" She was finding it harder and hard to say the word, "husband. Is there someone I can speak to about his upcoming release?"

"I'll page the resident," the blonde, pony-tailed young woman said. She looked as young as Cheryl. "You can go right in and visit him. The stimulation will do him good."

Sabina nodded, feeling just a little awkward. Did these nurses know about Courtney and that Sabina was the soon-to-be ex-wife? Nonetheless, the responsibility was on her, and Courtney was nowhere to be seen.

As Sabina entered the hospital room, Jonathan turned his head and looked at her with those familiar eyes. Sabina forced a smile, unsure of what to expect. He looked at her curiously, as though he recognized her but he didn't fully connect the pieces. Sabina walked over to him.

"Hello, Jonathan. It's good to see you awake."

A scrubs-clad woman walked in behind her, and as Sabina turned to face her, she caught a glimpse of Jonathan's hands. He held them stiffly at his sides, his fingers curled, with a slight twitch. The resident smiled at her.

"Hello, I'm Dr. Casey. You're Mrs. Miller?"

Sabina nodded. Yet another doctor? How was anyone

supposed to get well when it was always a stranger who saw them?

"It's good to meet you." The resident nodded in Jonathan's direction. "As you can see, your husband has improved significantly in the last forty-eight hours. Going to the rehab facility should help him regain his speech and the ability to walk."

Help? That word covered a lot of territory.

"I understand you made your choice of facilities."

Word traveled fast. They really wanted to be rid of Jonathan—and quickly.

"I wasn't given much choice," Sabina said evenly.

"Oh? I'm sorry to hear that."

"So am I." An awkward moment passed where the resident didn't seem to know where to look. Sabina saved her the embarrassment.

"In your opinion, is Jonathan likely to ever be able to practice law again?"

The resident hesitated. "That depends on the progress he makes in rehab."

Sabina had done some Internet research. "Physical as well as occupational therapy," she stated.

"Yes. When your husband arrives at the home, they'll evaluate him and decide where to concentrate their efforts. Many people *do* make a remarkable recovery from strokes," she said encouragingly.

Sabina looked at Jonathan, who, though awake, didn't seem to be taking in any of the conversation.

Sabina mustered a wan smile. "Thank you, doctor."

The woman nodded and pivoted to leave the room.

Sabina turned back to look at the man she once promised to love and cherish. "I'm sorry this happened, Jonathan. Hopefully, this is a turning point and you'll be back on your feet and ready to litigate once more."

Jonathan stared vacantly ahead.

Yeah, and pigs could fly.

Sabina left the floor and slowly made her way through the hospital. She knew what she had to do and wasn't looking forward to it. She was going to have to call Courtney. Maybe when she got to her car she wouldn't get a signal and she could put it off a couple of hours, but when she pulled out her phone, she was able to make the call to Jonathan's office.

"Bradly, Peterson, Holtz, and Miller. Mr. Miller's office. How can I help you?"

"Gretchen? It's Sabina."

"Mrs. Miller. It's so good to hear your voice. I hope you have good news for me—er, us."

Sabina stifled a smile. "As a matter of fact, I do. Jonathan has made enough progress that the hospital will be discharging him tomorrow."

"He's coming back to work?" Gretchen asked eagerly.

"I'm afraid not. They're transferring him to Apple Grove Senior Community Living Center tomorrow."

"That's...wonderful," Gretchen said, not sounding at all sure.

"I need to speak to Ms. Sullivan, but I don't have her direct number. Would you be able to transfer me to her office?"

"Of course. Um, before I do...would it be okay if I visited Mr. Miller at the senior center sometime?"

Considering how few visitors Jonathan had received so far... "I'm sure he'd enjoy hearing what's going on at the office."

"Oh, good. Thank you. Hang on a minute while I transfer you."

"Thank you."

After several seconds of dead air, the phone rang and was picked up.

"Courtney Sullivan."

"Courtney? It's Sabina."

"Oh. Hello," she said flatly.

"I'm calling to let you know that tomorrow Jonathan will be transferred to Apple Grove in Penfield for rehab."

"Rehab?" She sounded surprised. "But the last time I was there…"

"He's improved during the past couple of days."

"Really?" she sounded surprised.

"You haven't visited him lately?" Sabina asked, already knowing the answer.

"Well, I've…I've been busy."

Too busy to visit the man who dumped me for you?

"Well, I just thought I'd give you the courtesy of a call to let you know. You *will* want to be on hand when he gets there tomorrow, won't you?"

"I…I've got to work. But I could visit him in the evening."

"And tonight as well?"

"Uh…yeah, why not?"

Why not?

Sabina glanced in the rear-view mirror and was glad there was no one around to see her sour expression.

"How's everything at the house? Any problems."

"Uh, no."

"That's good. I'm sure Jonathan will rest better knowing you're taking such good care of it."

Silence.

"Well, I know you're busy so I'll let you go."

"Uh, thanks for calling. It was…nice of you."

"I'm sure we'll be in touch," Sabina said. "Goodbye."

She didn't wait for a reply.

With that taken care of, Sabina replaced her phone in her purse.

Like Courtney, she had a job—which she'd been sadly neglecting. Once Jonathan was in the rehab home she figured she could turn her full attention to Sabina Reigns Designs. After all, with so many mouths to feed, she had to make the business pay.

CHAPTER 25

*I*t was almost two when Sabina returned to her showroom. She'd stopped at the grocery store to grab a sandwich and a bottle of iced tea. What she really needed to do was do a real shopping haul and restock her cupboards, which were pretty empty after Marisa's visit, but she didn't have time that day. She needed to start cooking again. She'd been living on take-out meals and too much caffeine these past few weeks. What she needed was to establish a routine. Maybe now that Jonathan was heading for rehab, she could again start to live her life without him and his problems taking up so much of her time —time she needed to be productive.

Todd was busy with a couple of retail customers when she returned to the showroom. She showed him the bag and he gave her a nod as she retreated to her office to eat it.

As soon as she sat down, her phone rang. She looked at the caller ID and smiled.

"Hi, Steve."

"Hey, lady, what's up?"

"Good news. My ex is being transferred to rehab."

"Does that mean he's better."

"Only marginally, but hopefully I shouldn't have to spend all my waking hours worried I'm going to get a call I don't want to take."

"And Marisa's back in school?"

"Yes."

"Does that mean you're free for dinner?"

Sabina let out a breath. "I don't know. We did have a tragedy yesterday."

"But you just said Jonathan was better."

"Yes, but it's Zoey. She lost her baby."

"Oh, God. That's terrible."

"Yeah. Do you mind if I check in with Julie before I give you an answer? I was with them last night and they were both pretty shattered."

"Sure. I'll be around. Will you call me later?"

"Definitely," she said, smiling.

"Great. Talk to you later."

Sabina set her phone on the desk and proceeded to eat her much-delayed lunch. But she decided to only eat half...just in case she was able to have dinner with Steve. Would this constitute their second date, or did Thanksgiving have that honor? No. You don't share a date with five other people. But at this point, she didn't care if they went for a Big Mac and fries as long as they could spend more than thirty minutes without interruption.

The bell above the door in the showroom tinkled and a moment later Todd stood in the office doorway. "We just made another twenty-six bucks," he said cheerfully.

"All we need now is another five thousand nine hundred and seventy-four bucks and we've made the rent for the month."

"Aw, come on, Sabina. It's a start."

Sabina wrapped up what was left of her lunch. "Yes, it is. Are you ready to start on those mock-ups?"

"I got everything we need this morning."

"Fine. Why don't you set everything up on the big counter

and I'll be right with you? I just need to make a couple of fast calls."

"You got it, boss," Todd said and disappeared around the corner.

Sabina picked up her phone, scrolled through her contacts until she came to Julie's number. She tapped it and in seconds was rewarded with the sound of her best friend's voice.

"Hi, Sabina." Her tone was neutral.

"I was just calling to see how things are going."

"We're home. Zoey's lying on the couch, watching TV. She's been crying off and on, but as I've been doing the same thing, I guess that's kind of normal."

"Do you need anything?"

"No. I snuck out of the hospital this morning before they discharged her and hit the grocery store. We've got tubs of ice cream, three frozen pizzas which I can doctor up to taste home-made, and cookies and chocolate up the wazoo. We're good to go for a couple of days."

"Is it okay if I tell Marisa what happened? Is it okay if she calls you guys?"

"Sure. If Zoey isn't up to speaking with her, I can give her an update."

"Thanks. I thought I might come and visit you tomorrow or Friday—if that's okay."

"Make it Friday. I think Zoey needs a little more time. And we're seeing a grief counselor tomorrow. I'm betting there'll be a lot more tears—from both of us."

"Okay, Friday it is. I can bring lunch?"

"That sounds great. Thanks."

"How's everything on your end?" Julie asked.

"They're transferring Jonathan to a nursing home in Penfield tomorrow."

"Wow—that was fast."

"He's actually doing much better. He'll get more therapy there than at the hospital."

"And the prognosis?" Julie asked.

"Still too early to tell." Sabina told Julie about her phone call to Courtney.

"Wow—not showing a lot of love for Jonathan, is she?"

"Maybe she's just too immature to cope. Anyway, she's not my problem."

"As long as she's living in *your* house, she's *your* problem," Julie remarked.

"Unfortunately, you're right." Sabina looked at the clock in the kitchen beyond and sighed. "I need to get some work done."

"I hear you. I have a party to cater on Saturday. I'm just lucky this tragedy didn't happen on the weekend or I don't know what I would have done."

"If you need help, holler. You know I'm there—and I'm sure I could talk Todd into serving again. He looked so cute in an apron and chef's toque"

"I heard that," Todd hollered from the next room.

Sabina rolled her eyes. Next time she had a private conversation, she'd shut her office door. "Seriously, if you need help—don't hesitate to call."

"With Zoey unavailable, I will probably have to do just that."

"We'll talk more about it tomorrow or Friday, okay?"

"Sure thing. And thanks for calling. Love you," Julie said.

"Love you more," Sabina replied and they signed off.

Todd appeared in her doorway. "Did you really just volunteer me to work for Julie on Saturday?"

"Sort of. If you can't do it, you can't do it. She *will* pay you."

"Minimum wage," Todd muttered.

"Are you doing anything else on Saturday? Have a date for instance? Going to save the planet or cure cancer?"

"Not exactly," he admitted.

"They've suffered a terrible loss, and now—"

"Okay, okay!" Todd said, raising his hands in surrender. "You don't need to play the guilt card. As it happens, I'm *not* busy on Saturday. And if she saves me a few leftover canapés, I *might* consider working for her in a pinch."

"Magnanimous of you. And I'm sure I can arrange for a doggy bag for you," she said flatly. "Now, I have a couple more phone calls to make."

"Don't mind me," Todd said and pivoted. "I'm going back to doing my *real* job."

Sabina watched until he was out of sight, then closed her door. She was about to call Steve when her phone rang. She glanced at the caller ID and saw it was Marisa. She tapped the call-answer icon.

"Missy, I was just about to call you."

"What's this about Dad going to rehab? Why didn't you call me!" she demanded.

Sabina let out a breath. "As I said, I was just about to call you."

"You called Courtney," Marisa said accusingly.

That bitch. Did Courtney deliberately contact Marisa so that she could be the bearer of good news, making Sabina look like the mean mom once again?

"She hadn't been to see your father in a couple of days. He could use the company."

"*You* could visit him more often."

"Well, I haven't. Now, they'll be discharging Dad tomorrow. He'll be going to Apple Grove for rehab."

"Why aren't *you* taking care of him yourself?"

Sabina blinked at the phone in her hands for several moments. "Sweetheart, I couldn't possibly take care of him. He's being moved to a facility better suited to his needs."

Marisa's voice hardened. "A nursing home?"

Sabina chose her words carefully. "Yes, it's a nursing home, but your Dad is being sent there for their expertise in treating someone who's had a stroke."

"But *you're* his wife," she insisted.

That took Sabina by surprise. "Soon to be ex-wife. Sweetheart, we have to face the fact that your father may never be the man that any of us knew. He needs round-the-clock care. He needs to be in an assisted living home—at least for now."

"No, no, no! *You* married my father for better or for worse, and *you* should honor that vow."

Sabina stood her ground: she wasn't going to be bullied by her daughter. "Marisa, this is not your decision. I understand that you're under a lot of stress, but this is *my* decision and you're not going to make me feel guilty because I refuse to give up my entire life to take care of your father. I remind you that he cheated on me, got another woman pregnant, and then kicked me out of my own home. Him having a stroke does not take any of that away. Not to mention the fact that considering the cost of your father's care, I'm going to have to work even harder to support not just you and me, but your Dad, and possibly Courtney's baby."

"We're not poor."

"We have money in our accounts, but it won't last forever. You can be angry about this, that's fine, but again, it's not your choice."

"You took a vow that included the words in 'sickness and in health.'"

"And your father and I were in the process of getting a divorce. If anybody should be taking care of your Dad, it's Courtney."

"You just said she hasn't been visiting Dad. She doesn't know what to do there. She doesn't even know what to do with herself."

"That's not my worry," Sabina replied. Her statement was met with silence. She took a breath and tried to remain calm. "I know you love your Dad; I don't want that to change. But as I'm the one taking care of his affairs, I'll make sure he's in the best place possible to help him recover. You're an adult now and you need to start thinking and acting like one."

"What do you mean?" Marisa asked sullenly.

"When you're financially secure enough to support yourself, you're more than welcome to take your Dad out of that place and take care of him. But remember, it'll take a lot of money, and you won't be able to abandon him if it gets to be too hard."

Sabina didn't normally speak to Marisa in that manner, but with everything that had gone on over the last few days, she didn't have the patience for her daughter's selfishness. She also realized Marisa didn't know about Zoey's baby. She took a deep breath. "Sweetheart, a lot's happened in the last forty-eight hours."

"Now what?" Marisa groused.

"Zoey had some complications and ended up in the hospital yesterday."

"Is she okay?"

"Unfortunately, no. They couldn't save the baby."

"Oh my God," she cried, but then her tone hardened once more. "And when were you going to tell me *that?*"

"As I said, I was just about to call you."

Marisa's tone softened. "Poor Zoey. I'll have to go see her when I get back home—maybe this weekend."

"You should stay at school and study," Sabina advised. Besides, she really couldn't afford for Marisa to keep flying between Pittsburgh and Rochester—not that she envied driving that far during the winter months to pick her up or drop her off.

"I met a couple of other kids from the area. They were talking about driving up for the weekend if the weather's okay. I could always study in the car."

Which wasn't likely to happen.

"Well, keep me posted. But if the weather gets bad, you're staying put. Do I make myself clear?"

"Okay," Marisa grudgingly agreed. "I gotta go."

"I'll let you know about the home after they transfer your Dad there tomorrow?"

"You're going there with him?"

"I'll probably have to sign paperwork, so there's a good possibility."

"I hope it's not horrible," Marisa said, her voice so quiet it was almost a whisper.

"I hope so, too. I wasn't given much of a choice. But we can talk about that tomorrow after I visit the place."

"Okay."

"Now, try not to think about all this heavy stuff."

"Like that's going to happen," Marisa said sourly.

"I'll talk to you soon," Sabina promised.

"Tomorrow," Marisa ordered.

"Yes, tomorrow. Bye now."

Sabina set her phone down and blew out a breath, feeling exhausted, knowing she was going to have to go to the nursing home sometime during the next day and sign her financial future away.

Life really sucked sometimes.

CHAPTER 26

*S*abina sat in her office chair, staring at her now-quiet phone for long seconds. What a crappy day—and it was only half over. But there had been one bright spot—Steve's call. And he'd invited her out to dinner.

Tired of putting everyone else's needs above her own, Sabina scrolled through her contacts list and placed the call.

"Hey there," Sabina said once Steve had answered. She'd expected voice mail.

"Hi, yourself."

The silence hung between them.

"Okay, what's wrong now?" Steve asked, not judgmentally, but kindly and interested.

Sabina closed her eyes and let out a long, frustrated breath.

"Are you okay?" Steve asked.

"Not really," Sabina said, feeling dispirited because of everything that was going on with Jonathan, Marisa, Zoey, Julie—and even Courtney. "But just the sound of your voice brings me more joy than you can imagine."

"Does that mean we're on for dinner tonight?" Steve asked, a note of expectation in his voice.

"If you'll have me," Sabina said.

Steve laughed. "Oh, Lady, you don't know what you've just opened yourself up to."

Sabina's mouth quirked. "I think you underestimate me." She could envision his corresponding expression.

"So, what's your dining pleasure?" Steve asked.

"Comfort food. I'm in desperate need of it."

Steve's laugh was golden. "I know just the place. What time should I pick you up?"

"Six thirty," Sabina suggested.

"I'll see you at your place then."

"Great. I'm *really* looking forward to this," Sabina said, hoping she didn't sound too desperate.

"Me, too," Steve remarked. "Until then." He ended the call.

* * *

THE REST of the workday was pretty unremarkable. Sabina and Todd started the Parkview Manor mock-ups, and when twilight had captured the sky, they locked up and walked to their respective cars. "Have fun tonight!" Todd called. "Don't do anything I wouldn't do."

"Maybe—maybe not," Sabina answered as she pressed the button on her key fob to unlock the car's driver's-side door. She climbed inside, started the engine, and headed for home.

There was that word again. Her apartment was definitely *not* home in the traditional sense, but she wasn't sure that she ever wanted to live in the house Jonathan had asked her to leave—and where he'd brought his mistress. But it was a real possibility—if she could figure out how to remove Courtney from the premises. But that wasn't a priority. Yet. When she thought of the financial implications Courtney and her child could impose upon her she wanted to cry. Why in God's name should *she* be responsible for paying child support for Jonathan's love child—but it only looked like that could be in the cards *if* Courtney kept the baby, which didn't look likely. And that Marisa had even contemplated Sabina taking in that baby made her break out in a sweat. Hopefully, she'd nipped that idea in the bud, but by law, Marisa was an adult. What if she found herself a lawyer and pursued the idea despite Sabina's advice? The girl was headstrong enough to do just that.

Don't think about it, Sabina told herself and found herself steering toward the big pharmacy on the corner near her apartment. She pulled into the parking lot, switched off the engine, and stared at the double glass doors, half afraid of what she contemplated doing. It had been in the back of her mind since Steve had called her earlier in the day. She took a deep breath, pulled the key from the ignition, and exited her vehicle. Then she marched inside the store and read the signs overhead, changed her trajectory, and headed to the back of the store. She examined the products for sale, chose the most expensive—thinking it had to be the best and most effective—and headed for the sales counter. The young man on duty snickered as he rang up her sale, but Sabina held her head up high and paid in cash. No way did she want her purchase to be registered in her name on the store's database.

Sabina headed for home—er, the awful little apartment, that was wasn't home but wasn't as hellish as she'd once considered it.

Once inside, she considered the items that hung in her closet —deciding all of them were hideous and choosing the least hideous of all—and changed clothes. Next, she worked on her hair and make-up. She was as nervous as a teenager going on a first date. Technically, this was her second date with Steve, but she wanted it to be special. She deserved a special time away from the mayhem in her life, and she was determined to get it.

Now, all she had to worry about was what Steve would bring to the occasion.

She set candles out on the coffee table, made sure there was a bottle of wine chilling in the fridge, and that the two wineglasses she owned were clean, and sat down to wait.

The last time Steve had taken her to dinner turned out to be a disaster, but Jonathan was now stable, Marisa was away at school, and Julie had asked her to give them another day to heal. The only blip on the radar was Todd, but he'd seemed to be in her court when it came to her dating journey. Unless her parents—snowbirds in Florida—had a problem, she might just have one blessed, peaceful night…and maybe more.

At precisely six thirty, Sabina's doorbell rang.

Ready or not, she got up and opened the door.

"I hope you checked to make sure it was me," Steve admonished her.

"I'm a responsible woman," Sabina declared, but who else would have been standing behind her door right on schedule?

Steve stepped inside and closed the door. "Are you ready?"

"I just have to get my coat." Sabina pulled it out of the tiny entryway closet, grabbed her purse, and gestured toward the door.

Steve led the way to his beat-up Ford pickup. Should she consider it a come-down from Jonathan's top-of-the-line Mercedes, or that of a humble man who didn't have a problem with who he was?

She chose the latter.

Instead of taking her to a fancy restaurant, Steve drove into the parking lot of a diner in Henrietta. Sabina was just a tad over-dressed for such an establishment and Steve seemed to read her mind.

"You said you wanted comfort food," he reminded her.

She had indeed.

The place seemed to welcome Sabina with its charming 1950s vibe, the black-and-white color scheme, and the clock encircled with pink neon and a sign that promised an endless cup of coffee. Once seated in one of the booths, Sabina was surprised to find the restaurant also contained a fully stocked bar.

"Can I get you something besides water to drink?" the waitress asked as she placed a couple of menus on the table.

Steve nodded in Sabina's direction.

"Whiskey and ginger ale."

Steve laughed. "Ah, whiskey pop. That's what my sister calls it."

"And you, sir?" the waitress asked.

"Scotch on the rocks."

She nodded and left them alone.

Sabina didn't bother to look at the menu. She wasn't going to be ready to order for a while. What she needed now was conversation. And not from Todd, or Julie, or Marisa. She craved something totally different.

"Tell me about your current project," she told Steve. "I want to know everything about it."

Steve was only happy to comply. He waxed on and on about sheathing, roof tiles, and plumbing, and Sabina listened with intent interest. Her trade was embellishing structures after they were made sound, but she never tired of hearing about the underpinnings of a restoration or reconstruction. Jonathan had never had the patience to listen to her talk about her work, but Steve was honestly interested when she spoke about the Parkview Manor restoration. And he'd actually driven out to the site to have a look.

"Seems like all they need now is a fresh coat of paint and some new landscaping."

"And they can't do that until at least May," she said. "Once we get approval for the inside remodel, it'll take place over the next five months. The house should be ready to reopen on or before Memorial Day.

"Then what will you do?"

Sabina laughed. "Be a guest at the grand opening—where I

will drink champagne, bask in the accolades, and press my business card into the hands of everyone I meet."

Steve grinned. "You're a woman after my own heart. But I can tell by the set of your jaw that there's a lot more going on."

Sabina wasn't sure if she should laugh or cry. Instead, she gulped the last of her drink.

The waitress returned and they ordered a fresh round and their meals. Sabina settled for the meatloaf, mashed potatoes, and gravy, and Steve ordered a steak.

It took the entire meal for her to catch him up on all her personal drama. "I wouldn't be surprised if you decide to dump me at my apartment and run away forever."

Steve shook his head. "We're at a stage in life where we're trapped between our kids and elderly parents. There's a reason they call it the sandwich generation. I don't envy your potential financial situation."

"It really burns me that I could be responsible for Jonathan's love child for the next eighteen years. I'm praying Courtney gives that baby up for adoption. Meanwhile, Marisa thinks I'm a heartless bitch. She has no clue what she was asking of me."

Steve nodded.

The waitress returned with the check along with a container for Sabina's leftovers, and Steve pulled out his wallet, placing several bills in the Naugahyde folder.

As they left the restaurant, it began to snow. "It looks like winter has arrived," Sabina said and sighed.

"It's that time of year," Steve agreed.

They were quiet on the drive to Sabina's place, and she wondered if they were both thinking the same thing: that this was the time to take their relationship to the next level. She was ready. It had been a long, lonely few years since she'd enjoyed making love. It was hard to muster enthusiasm when you suspected our spouse of cheating. And, damn! Why hadn't she just come out and asked Jonathan?

Because she had a teenager in high school. She hadn't wanted to disrupt Marisa's life. But if she had, they might have been through the whole separation and divorce. She could have started her business a year or more sooner. Her new *life* could have started sooner.

Steve pulled up outside of Sabina's apartment.

"Would you like to come in for a nightcap?" she asked.

He grinned. "That sounds like a prelude to seduction."

She frowned. "In your dreams." *You mind reader, you.* "I thought after that well-seasoned steak that you might be thirsty."

"Now that you mention it, I think I am."

Sabina gave him a sly smile and opened the car door, letting herself out.

Steve followed her to her apartment door. After unlocking it, Sabina led the way in. She hung up her coat, and Steve did likewise.

"Come in and sit down. I hope you like Chardonnay."

"I prefer beer, but I've been known to kill a bottle now and then."

Sabina made a mental note: *try to find out his favorite brew.* Maybe Todd would know. She'd ask him.

Steve settled on the couch while Sabina puttered in the kitchen, putting away her leftovers and bringing out the glasses and the good corkscrew she'd lifted from her former kitchen. Jonathan wasn't much of a wine drinker and she guessed he'd never miss it. Being pregnant, Courtney shouldn't be drinking—whether she did wasn't Sabina's business. And if Courtney was imbibing, she could buy a new one—or rely on screw-top bottles.

Sabina entered the living room and handed Steve a glass. "I'm sorry I don't have any music, I had a wonderful system in the old house, but I left it behind."

Steve looked around the room. "You only have that dinky TV."

Sabina shrugged and sat down beside him. "I needed to have

something for Marisa when she visits. I don't watch it much," she said.

"But you've got that big TV in the showroom."

"As a prop. If I want to see something or listen to background music, there are a lot of Internet sites I can watch or listen to on my phone or laptop."

"With shitty sound quality," he remarked and took a sip of wine."

Sabina looked around her far-from-optimum surroundings and sighed. "I've learned to live with it."

"I feel bad that you have to," Steve said with what sounded like regret.

Sabina smiled. "I've got what I wanted most; my freedom and my business."

"Are you free?" Steve asked, his expression sober.

Her smile faded. "No, I'm not. I'm still tethered to Jonathan and those entanglements may get worse." But then she gave herself a shake. "I don't want to think about it—at least, not tonight. Why don't we forget about work, other people, and just enjoy each other's company?"

Steve gazed into her eyes and then leaned forward, placing a gentle kiss on her lips. He pulled back, giving her a reassuring smile.

"Thank you for dinner. It was nice. Just what I needed."

"What else do you need, Sabina?" he asked, his voice sounding husky.

She offered him a crooked grin. "I think you know."

Steve shook his head. "I didn't come prepared."

"Then it's a good thing I am," Sabina said. She set her wine glass down, stood, and offered him her hand. "Come with me."

Steve accepted, and Sabina led him to the bedroom.

CHAPTER 27

*S*omewhere in the middle of the night, Sabina woke a little disoriented until she realized she was nestled in Steve's arms. She wrapped her arm around his and fell back asleep.

Sometime later, she was awakened by the sound of rustling. She rolled over in bed and saw Steve sitting on the side of the bed, pulling on a sock.

"Hey, sleepyhead. Rise and shine."

Sabina squinted at the glowing scarlet numerals on her bedside clock. "But it's only six o'clock."

"I start work at seven—you start at ten. Go back to sleep," he told her.

"And let you leave without breakfast?"

He finished dressing. "What have you got in the fridge?"

Sabina frowned. "Stale pizza and leftover meatloaf and potatoes."

Steve smiled. "I'll take a raincheck. How about this weekend?"

Sabina remembered that Marisa had threatened to come home from school to visit Jonathan and Zoey. She frowned. "Maybe. Maybe not," she said and explained.

Steve stood and walked to the other side of the bed. He leaned down and kissed Sabina. "We'll figure it out."

She smiled and kissed him again.

"I've gotta go. Mrs. Morrow's kitchen awaits me."

"Okay."

He turned for the bedroom door and Sabina got up, grabbing her robe and tying the belt around her waist as she followed him into the living room. "Are you sure I can't at least make you a cup of coffee."

"I've got to get my tools. I'll grab one along the way."

Steve shrugged into his jacket and gave her one last kiss before he was out the door. She moved to the window and watched as he got in the truck and started the engine. At least the snow hadn't accumulated overnight so he didn't have to scrape off the windshield. She waved as he pulled out of the parking space and out of the lot.

Now that she was up, Sabina decided she may as well stay up and make a pot of coffee. While it brewed, she checked her phone. She'd missed a text from the hospital. A medi-cab was set to pick Jonathan up at two that afternoon. Could she come in to sign yet more paperwork around one?

Yes, she could.

Sabina had a feeling it was going to be a very long day.

WITH EVERYTHING that awaited her that afternoon, Sabina had a feeling she wasn't going to get back to the showroom that afternoon so she drank her coffee, showered and dressed, grabbed her doggy bag, and hit the road just after seven. At least she'd have several hours of peace to check on the inventory they'd sold and decide if she could afford to order more. And she'd save money on lunch with her leftovers from the evening before.

Todd arrived fifteen minutes before opening, offering a bag of still-warm bagels.

"How did you know I didn't have breakfast?" Sabina asked.

"You never eat breakfast at home."

"That's because my fridge is always empty. Hand over the receipt, buster, and I'll reimburse you from petty cash."

"Whatever you say," Todd said, handed over the slip, and hung up his coat before getting out a couple of plates, knives, and the cream cheese from the fridge. "We could save a lot of money if we just bought some groceries for here and had breakfast together every day. It could be a bonding experience. What do you say?"

Sabina squinted up at him. "First, are you sure you're not gay?"

Todd laughed. "Positive. Why?"

"Because you're one of the most thoughtful guys I've ever met."

"Then you've been traveling with the wrong crowd."

Sabina nodded. "Okay, let's do it. With my soon-to-be precarious financial situation, I need to save money wherever I can."

They took their breakfasts to the showroom's dining room area and sat at the big table.

"I hope you're okay holding the fort—again—this afternoon because I need to go to the hospital to sign the paperwork for Jonathan's discharge and then follow the medi-cab to the nursing home where I get to potentially sign away my entire future earnings."

"Maybe it'll only be temporary and Jonathan will improve so fast they'll discharge him before Easter," Todd offered optimistically.

Easter was four months away. At nearly ten grand a month, that was a lot of maybes.

"We'll see," Sabina said and took a bite of her bagel.

* * *

SABINA SIGNED the last piece of paper, pushing the pile back toward the social worker.

"That's everything. Now, all we have to do is wait for the medi-cab to come to pick up Mr. Miller and take him to rehab." Cheryl Dawson positively grinned.

Sabina felt no such joy—for herself or Jonathan.

"Why don't you wait for them to arrive in his room, then you can follow them to the home."

It had taken an hour of her time just to get things set up on this end. How long would it take once she got to the facility in Penfield?

Cheryl stood and offered her hand. "It was so nice meeting you, Mrs. Miller."

The last thing Sabina wanted to do was shake on such a deal, but she had been brought up to practice certain amenities.

Sabina left the cramped office and made her way up to Jonathan's room. Of course, there was no sign of Courtney.

The door to Jonathan's room was open. The bed had been raised so that he sat up, but his condition didn't seem to have changed from the day before.

"Hello, Jonathan. How are you today?" she asked.

Jonathan didn't answer, but he gave a twitch. Was he reacting to the sound of her voice?

"You'll be heading for rehab any time now. They'll help get you back in shape. Gretchen said she might come and visit you there. Won't it be nice to hear what's going on at the firm?"

Jonathan gave another shudder.

And what should she say now?

Sabina pulled the uncomfortable chair closer to the bed. The TV was off, but the control lay on the bed near Jonathan's right hand. She could turn the set on and kill time by watching HGTV until the medi-cab arrived. She could check her phone for messages, although she was sure Todd could handle just about anything that came up back at the showroom.

Movement to her left caused her to look up. Jonathan's body had stiffened and his limbs twitched uncontrollably.

Sabina launched to her feet and ran for the door.

"Help!" she called. "I think my husband's having a seizure!"

Two of the nurses shot around their station and ran for the room. Sabina watched as several other professionals followed them in. The charge nurse grabbed for the door handle and glanced at Sabina. "Please wait outside."

Feeling panicked, Sabina hurriedly stepped into the corridor. She stood, restlessly shifting her weight from one foot to the other and biting her lip. As much as Jonathan had hurt her, she didn't want him to suffer—for his sake, and more importantly for Marisa's.

Sabina fought the urge to take out her phone and call...who? Julie? Courtney? Definitely not her daughter. Not yet. Not until she knew what was going on.

Suddenly a voice called over the public address system: "Code Blue" on that floor—in fact, Jonathan's room! Sabina had seen enough medical TV shows to know what that meant: Jonathan's condition had suddenly turned life-threatening.

Almost immediately, the corridor was filled with medical personnel, with one scrubs-clad man pushing what could only be a cardio crash cart. He rushed inside the room and the door was closed once more.

How many people were crammed into that room to work on Jonathan?

Sabina kept her gaze riveted on Jonathan's door. The minutes ticked away. She was vaguely aware of the visitors coming and going, techs visiting patient rooms pushing their little machines that checked blood pressure and oxygen intake, and workers collecting the lunch trays and pushing the noisy carts toward the service elevators.

And Sabina waited, finally noticing her fingernails had dug deep ruts into her palms.

Don't panic, she kept telling herself over and over again. But the longer she waited, the more anxious she became.

It felt like hours, but she knew by the clock at the nurses' station that it had only been some forty minutes since all hell had broken loose in Jonathan's room.

Finally, the door opened and a haggard-looking man in blue scrubs emerged with one of the nurses behind him. She pointed at Sabina, whispered something to him before he walked over to join Sabina.

"I'm Dr. Powell—"

Yet another *doctor*? Sabina thought with dismay.

"I've been told that you're Mr. Miller's wife."

Sabina nodded. "Yes. What happened?"

The doctor took in a deep breath, his gaze shifting around the corridor before meeting hers. He cleared his throat "Mr. Miller suffered a seizure and lost consciousness. I'm sorry to tell you that he then went into cardiac arrest. We did our best but were unsuccessful reviving Mr. Miller."

"He's dead," Sabina stated. She could tell by the man's expression what his answer would be.

He nodded.

Sabina took in a deep breath and closed her eyes for a moment as a rush of pain and anxiety streaked through her. In her mind's eye, she saw Jonathan's face—the face she saw when she walked down the aisle twenty years before to marry him. She had to remind herself that the Jonathan she had fallen in love with was gone even before he had a stroke.

She rubbed a hand across her face before looking back at the doctor. "Thank you for trying to save him."

He nodded. "Of course. You're welcome to stay with him, along with any other family or friends you want to call, and for as long as you need to."

"Thank you," Sabina managed to say. Oddly enough, the fear had evaporated. Now all she felt was empty.

"I'll have the social worker come and talk to you. There are decisions that need to be made."

"I understand." Oh yeah...Julie had just gone through the same thing for Robin.

"I'm so sorry," Dr. Powell said.

Again, Sabina nodded and once again found herself thanking the man.

Powell turned to leave and Sabina stood in the hallway watching as the rest of the hospital personnel quietly filed out of Jonathan's room, once again closing the door.

It took Sabina another minute or two to work up the courage to enter the room. What was she likely to find?

Jonathan was dead.

Accepting the finality of those words was nearly too much to bear.

She had loved him. Made a home with him. Had a daughter with him. She'd lived half of her life with him, and now he was gone.

For a moment—*a moment*—she forgot all the pain he had caused her and Marisa, remembering only the love they'd once shared.

Mustering her courage, Sabina entered the deathly quiet room.

The nurses must have tidied up, for Jonathan lay on the bed, the hospital gown covering his chest and the sheet pulled up to his waist, his arms resting on top. She stepped closer.

He's dead.

Sabina studied his now lax face.

"Well, what happens now?" Sabina asked the man on the bed.

She knew Jonathan's wishes. They'd talked about it several times throughout their marriage. Not that either of them thought it would happen for decades. He wanted to be cremated and his ashes spread somewhere beautiful at sunset. Perhaps on a hillside near the sea. They'd spent their honeymoon in Maine and had taken several vacations there as well. Sabina realized it would be up to her to decide where and when—with Marisa's input, of course.

Marisa! How was she going to break the news to her daughter?

Sabina touched Jonathan's right hand, which hadn't yet gone cold, making lazy circles with her fingers against his skin. Then she leaned down and kissed his forehead.

She straightened.

"Goodbye, Jonathan."

And then, sad but dry-eyed, she stepped out of the room and shut the door behind her.

CHAPTER 28

It felt so odd to pull up the drive to her old home. The first thing Sabina noticed was that Jonathan's car was parked in the yard at the far side of the garage. He never left his car out of the garage overnight. Courtney had access to his keys, had she been driving it?

Sabina got out of her car. It galled her that she had to knock on the front door of the home she still technically owned. Hell, unless Jonathan had changed the locks, Sabina still had the keys to all the doors.

Knocking did no good. There were lights on inside the house, so presumably, Courtney was inside. Sabina pressed the doorbell. After no one appeared, she pressed it again—this time for a count of ten. She waited another thirty seconds, and when it wasn't answered. She pressed on the bell for twenty seconds. Finally, she heard the thud of footsteps. It took another four or five seconds —presumably for Courtney to look through the door's peephole —for it to open.

"Why are you here?" Courtney asked briskly.

"May I come in?" Sabina asked.

Courtney threw a glance over her shoulder before answering.

"I guess." She stepped aside, begrudgingly letting Sabina enter.

Her first look at the entryway gave Sabina a start. Since she'd left the property two months before, it had been painted a hideous shade of brown. As she looked beyond, she could see the living room had undergone another color change—this a dark blue, which clashed with all the furniture that still resided in the room.

"Why are you here?" Courtney pressed.

"May we sit?" Sabina asked.

Courtney let out what sounded like an exasperated short. "I suppose." Being six-months pregnant, she waddled her way into the living room and eased herself into what used to be Sabina's favorite chair. "What's so important that you had to bother me?" Courtney asked shortly.

Sabina steeled herself before answering. "I didn't want you to find out by other means," she said, not sure how else to begin. "I'm very sorry to have to tell you but...Jonathan had another medical emergency earlier today."

Courtney's eyes widened. "And you're only just telling me this now?" she shrieked.

"I'm sorry. I was at the hospital signing the paperwork to have him transferred to rehab when he suffered a seizure."

"What are you trying to tell me?" Courtney demanded angrily.

Sabina looked at the fourth finger of her left hand, where her wedding band used to reside. "Jonathan died of cardiac arrest this afternoon."

Sabina had expected tears—keening perhaps—but instead, Courtney's expression contorted into a scowl. "He's dead?"

"Yes, I'm afraid so. I haven't even told Marisa. I don't know how I'm going to break the news to her. But as Jonathan's fiancé, I thought you should be told."

Courtney's head dipped to take in her belly. Sabina also noted that she was rubbing her ring finger with her left thumb: a finger which no longer sported the big, sparkling rock Jonathan had given her. Now, neither of them wore the symbols of commitment to the man.

A bang from above caused both women to look up. It sounded like something heavy had been dropped. Sabina turned her expectant gaze toward Courtney, but the younger woman offered no explanation.

Sabina stood. "I have to get going. I need to go to Pittsburgh to let Marisa know about Jonathan. At least she'll miss him." Sabina turned away.

"What's that supposed to mean?" Courtney asked, sharply.

Sabina didn't answer. Instead, as she headed for the door, she called over her shoulder, "I'll let you know about the arrangements. I'm sure you'll want to be there for Jonathan's funeral."

She opened the front door and fought the urge to slam it behind her. As she headed for the driveway, she stopped to peer into the garage window. Two cars were parked inside: Courtney's Hyundai and a stranger's car.

As she pulled out of the driveway, Sabina looked up and saw the silhouette of a man peeking through the master bedroom's drapes.

Somehow, Sabina wasn't surprised.

During the drive back to her apartment, Sabina considered her options. She could call the resident advisor in Marisa's dorm and give her a heads up about the phone call. She would know who Missy hung out with or if she was close to her roommate. Or she could fly to Pittsburgh and deliver the news in person.

No way would she want to find out such devastating news via a phone call, but there was no way she could get to Pittsburgh until late morning or early afternoon the following day.

Of course, there was a third alternative.

Upon entering her apartment, she shrugged out of her coat and pulled her phone out of her purse, taking a seat at the peninsula. She scrolled through her contacts and tapped one to make a call.

"Yesirree, boss lady. What's with calling me on my own time, you slave driver you," Todd joked.

"I'm sorry. You always put in your time and you're cheerful about pushing the limits. I don't know what I'd do without you."

"What's wrong?" Todd asked, all the levity drained from his tone.

"Jonathan died a little while ago."

"Oh my God. Marisa's going to be devastated."

"I know. I have to drive to Pittsburgh to give her the news in person."

"Not alone, you won't."

"Julie can't leave Zoey, and I—"

"We'll go together. You know I'd do anything for Marisa."

"That's what I'm afraid of," Sabina remarked.

"Sabina," Todd warned.

"I'm sorry. You made me a promise and I know you won't go back on your word."

"That's right." Todd paused before speaking. "I can be at your place in twenty minutes. It's only a five-hour drive, but you don't want to be exhausted when you deliver the news. I'll make a reservation at a motel so we can crash for a few hours. Does that sound okay?"

For the first time that day, Sabina was reduced to tears. "I don't know what I'd do without you Todd. Thank you."

"Okay. Keep it together," he advised. "Pack a bag, and I'll see in you twenty minutes."

"Thank you," she said again and they ended the call.

Sabina did as he'd advised, packed some clean clothes, a few cosmetics, and had her bag waiting by the door. She still had at least ten minutes. She picked up her phone and made a call.

"Hey, Sabina, what's up?" Julie asked, sounding just as weary as Sabina felt.

"I'm afraid I don't have much time or good news. But first, tell me how Zoey's doing."

"As well as can be expected. There were a lot of tears at our first therapy session. She's going to join group therapy next week, but I'll keep going with her for as long as our insurance will allow it. Now, what's this bad news you've got to tell me?"

Sabina let out a long breath. "Jonathan died this afternoon."

"But you said he was better yesterday," Julie accused. "What happened?"

"He had a seizure and then a massive heart attack. They couldn't bring him back."

"Oh, gosh. Well, it looks like you saved a bundle on that nursing home."

"Julie!" Sabina chided her.

"I know, I know. I'm sorry."

Sabina felt a stab of guilt. She'd already thought of that, too.

"Todd'll be here any minute to get me. We're driving to Pittsburgh to tell Missy."

"Oh, gosh. She'll be devastated. How about Courtney?"

"I already broke the news to her. She *wasn't* devastated. In fact, she's apparently harboring a man—in *my* home!"

"*Now* can you evict the bitch?"

"I don't know. Squatters' rights and all. That's another thing I need to call Tonya about. Courtney could still sue for child support—if she decides to keep the baby. I'm sure Jonathan didn't put anything in writing for Courtney, at least I hope to God he didn't."

A beam of light flashed in front of the curtain-covered front window.

"I think Todd's here. I've gotta go."

"Call or text me."

"Will do."

"I love you," Julie said.

"Love you more," Sabina told her and ended the call.

Sabina turned off the lights, grabbed her duffel, and headed out the door.

CHAPTER 29

For the most part, the drive along the New York State Thruway heading west and then south to Pennsylvania was quiet. At first, Sabina and Todd traded life stories, but they'd long since run out of things to say by the time they hit the Pennsylvania State line and started down I-79.

Sabina tried to stay awake during the long ride in the dark but found her head snapped back every time she started to doze. Todd turned on the radio for company.

It was after midnight when Todd pulled up to a neat-looking, four-story motel in a suburb outside of Pittsburgh. "I got us a sweet deal on a suite," he said.

"Oh, but that's so expensive," Sabina protested

"Not when I've got credit card points to pay for it."

"I *will* be reimbursing you for the full value."

"Of course," he said matter-of-factly.

They grabbed their stuff and headed into the smart-looking lobby, which had a charming gas fireplace burning brightly, comfortable upholstered seating, and beyond it, an inviting breakfast room decorated simply but elegantly. Sabina was impressed, which was saying something. And at least they wouldn't have to go searching for food at the dawn's early light.

The rooms were just as attractive. Clean, comfortable, and with a small galley kitchen and a living room with a couch, a coffee table, and a large-screen TV. Each bedroom boasted a queen size bed with sumptuous linens, a private bath, and, fluffy terry robes for the guests to use. Not bad at all. Sabina might even have enjoyed the experience if it weren't for what she had to face in the morning.

She changed into her flannel pajamas, hit the bed, and was instantly asleep. When she awoke the next morning, the bedside clock told her it was nearly seven. She wanted to be at the college dorm before nine when Marisa would leave for her first class. On the day Jonathan had announced his desire for a divorce, he'd wanted Sabina to toss every piece of paper that had been stuck to the fridge with magnets. She'd taken everything down that very day and saved it all—and was glad that one of the rescued items had been her daughter's class schedule.

They went down to have breakfast around seven thirty. Todd tucked into eggs, bacon, sausage, toast, and coffee. Sabina had no appetite and settled for coffee and a small sweet roll, but then found she could only eat half of it. They were packed and on the road half an hour later.

Traffic was heavier than they'd anticipated and it was quarter to nine when Todd pulled up to the guest parking lot. It was a bit of a hike to Marisa's dorm, and already a throng of students were on their way to classes. Sabina bit her lip and hoped they hadn't already missed her daughter. She didn't want to call to let her know they were on-site, but if she had to, she could text and ask where Marisa was and what she was up to without giving away their location.

Sabina had only been on campus one other time. Jonathan had gone on the scouting trip with their daughter, and Marisa had been fine to leave her mom back home to fume in silence.

But Sabina and Marisa had actually done some bonding while choosing the decorations, bedding, and supplies the girl would need for her first real time away from home.

While Todd waited in the dorm's lobby, Sabina checked in with the residents' adviser and gave her a quick rundown of why she was there. The RA agreed to take her to Marisa's floor. Before she could knock on the suite's door, it opened and Marisa and another student stood before them.

When Marisa saw Sabina in the hallway, her face crumpled and she immediately broke down.

She knew.

Sabina stepped forward, took her daughter in her arms, and held her as though she were a child again. Unfortunately, she couldn't make this situation better.

"What happened?" Marisa managed despite her sobs.

"Let's go back to your dorm room," Sabina suggested.

"I'll see you later," the other girl told Marisa, patted her shoulder, and headed down the corridor.

Another girl sat on the couch in the common area, the TV blaring while she ate what looked like a burrito and consulted her phone.

Marisa led Sabina into her dorm room and shut the door. The only place to sit was on Marisa's bed, which was unmade. A box of tissues sat on a small table that held Missy's childhood jewelry box and a teddy bear that had been Marisa's companion through most of her teen years.

Sabina pushed back the comforter and they sat side-by-side on the mattress.

"Daddy's dead, isn't he?" Marisa cried.

"Yes, baby, he's gone."

"What? How?"

"He had a seizure and that brought on a massive heart attack. I was there at the hospital when it happened."

"Then at least he didn't die alone."

Sabina couldn't tell her girl that she hadn't been with Jonathan when he passed, but she could give her a truthful answer. "No, baby, he didn't die alone."

Marisa's tears still flowed freely, but she nodded, gaining some kind of solace. "We have to go home. I need to see him."

"Are you sure you want to do that?" Sabina asked.

Marisa nodded, wiping at a tear that rolled down her cheek. She looked around the messy dorm room. "I just wanna go home."

Except that Marisa's home was still held hostage by Courtney. "Of course. Come on."

Sabina stood, offered her hand, and pulled her daughter upright. They didn't bother packing a thing. Arm in arm, Sabina and Marisa left the dorm

They met Todd in the lobby, and Marisa rushed to him, throwing her arms around him. He looked at Sabina as though asking permission to return the hug. She nodded, and Todd wrapped his arms around Marisa, patting her back as she cried.

After a while, Marisa pulled back. Sabina stood ready with a fresh tissue. Then the three of them walked to the car.

Todd started the engine, pulled out of the lot, and headed north.

* * *

SATURDAY MORNING ROLLED AROUND and Sabina opened her eyes to take in a sea of tawny hair spread across the pillow next to hers. It took her a moment to remember the awful events of the day before. Telling Marisa about Jonathan's death, the long silent drive home, and then the trip to the funeral parlor.

Marisa decided not to view Jonathan's body, which was a relief for Sabina. She wanted to "remember him as he was." They tearfully made the arrangements, and when the funeral director suggested a keepsake piece of jewelry that held a tiny portion of cremains, Marisa chose a filigree tree of life design in sterling silver. "Think of it as your dad's last gift to you," Sabina said as Marisa nodded, wiping away more tears. They decided to wait a day or so to decide on a day for the funeral.

Sabina hauled herself out of bed and hit the shower. She had to nag Marisa to get up, but they'd made plans the evening before. It would be a long, busy day—at least for Sabina.

It was after ten when Sabina dropped Marisa off at Julie's house. She stopped in to check on Zoey, who was overjoyed to see not only Marisa, but the bags filled with movies, snacks, games, coloring books, and colored pencils and crayons. The two unhappy girls would keep busy that day, too.

After that, Sabina drove to the commercial kitchen where she knew Julie would be hard at work. She parked the car and walked across the lot. When a couple of knocks didn't produce any effect, she pounded on the steel door.

A tearful Julie answered, her mouth dropping open as she lunged forward to hug Sabina. "You're here!"

"Of course I am. I promised to help you with tonight's catering job, didn't I?"

"Yes, but with everything's that happened, I figured there was no way..."

"I wouldn't let you down, Jules. Now, let me in, willya? It's cold out here."

CHAPTER 30

"*J*'m so sorry for your loss," said Jonathan's grief-stricken secretary, Gretchen, holding Marisa's hands in hers. "Your father was a *wonderful* man."

Marisa nodded and averted her bloodshot, puffy eyes. Of all the people who'd arrived to pay their respects, it seemed only Marisa and Gretchen would truly miss Jonathan.

The funeral service had been sparsely attended, but droves of Jonathan's co-workers, and his partners and their wives, had made it to the reception at their home afterward. Sabina wasn't keen on hosting it, but Marisa needed the closure and she didn't want to deny her that small comfort.

Sabina stood to one side, holding a wine glass, studying the crowd.

Julie ambled up, leaned in, and muttered, "I can't believe you used to be friends with all these people. They look like such assholes."

Sabina raised an eyebrow.

"Uh, pretentious, that's the word I was looking for."

Sabina smiled. "They were never my friends. Their sympathetic words are nothing more than empty platitudes. I'm pretty sure every single one of them knew that Jonathan was cheating on me with Courtney."

"Shall I yell fire to disperse them?" Julie suggested.

"I'm sure most of them will leave soon anyway."

"Just pull out the cheap wine and you'll see them leave almost immediately."

Sabina laughed, knowing full well that she was probably right.

"Speaking of Courtney," Julie said, looking around the room. "She hasn't made an appearance. Doesn't she live here?"

Sabina shrugged. "I'm not surprised she isn't here. Before we went to the funeral parlor, I tried to talk to her about how she should participate, but she didn't want anything to do with it. In fact, she showed very little emotion at all."

"That's *cold*," Julie said.

"And, yes, she *does* live here. Her things are still in the master bedroom. I peeked. I suppose it was kind that she permitted us to hold the reception here at the house, although legally I don't suppose I needed it."

"Marisa must be a master of persuasion," Julie said and scowled.

Sabina shrugged. "I guess everyone handles grief in their own way, although I think Courtney has been preparing for a life without Jonathan since the moment he went to the hospital."

Julie scoffed. "True love. Zoey wasn't fond of Jonathan, but she asked me to send her apologies for not being here."

"She has nothing to apologize for. Two funerals in a week—who could blame her. How's she doing?"

Julie shrugged. "I'm glad her friend, Amy, came over to be with her while I'm here. I don't like leaving her alone for too long. She gets all weepy and depressed. Amy's a character and is helping Zoey to catch up with some schoolwork."

"Will she go back after Christmas vacation?"

Julie nodded. "I thought it might be too soon, but Zoey says she's ready. She sure has grown up these past few weeks." Julie looked away and swallowed. Sabina patted her friend's arm in solidarity.

Todd was getting good at playing server and scooted up next to Sabina holding a near-empty tray of Julie's famous bacon-wrapped scallops. He offered them to Sabina, but she waved a hand to beg off. "I can't believe you gave this house up."

"It was for the greater good," she reminded Todd.

He rolled his eyes in the direction of the foyer. "I can't say the color scheme is my taste, but it has so much to work with," Todd continued.

Sabina shook her head. "Jonathan's former, soon to be baby mama came in and repainted everything in these hideous shades. Either I fought him for the house or getting my business."

Todd nodded toward Marisa who looked like she wanted to escape from Gretchen. She smiled kindly at him and then scowled at Sabina before turning away. Todd winced. "What's going on?"

Sabina took another sip of her wine, staring over the edge of the glass at her daughter. "We argued before the service."

Todd and Julie both raised an eyebrow. "About what?"

Sabina frowned. "Courtney's been talking about putting her baby up for adoption. At first, Marisa wanted to become the legal guardian, but I pointed out the fact that she doesn't even have a job, or her own place, or the use of a car that's not in her father's name. I don't think she's given up the idea of her becoming the baby's guardian and me supporting them both."

"That's pretty brazen of her," Julie replied. "To ask your mother to take care of the child that was conceived by cheating on you."

Sabina nodded. "Exactly. Missy will be leaving the nest in a few years. There's no way that I want to be tied down with a baby at this stage of my life—not when I finally have my independence."

Several people started moving toward the front door. Sabina

handed her glass to Julie. I'd better go make like a hostess and thank them for coming."

"Better you than me," Julie muttered and turned to pick up another discarded glass and headed for the kitchen.

When all the guests had left, Sabina, Todd, and Julie went into total clean-up mode and suddenly Marisa was nowhere to be found. She mentioned she might poke around in the attic to find some pictures. Well, it sounded good, anyway.

Sabina had just hauled the vacuum into the middle of the living room when the front door opened. Sabina craned her neck to see who had arrived far-too-late for the reception and wasn't surprised to see it was Courtney, followed by a good-looking guy, six feet tall with slicked-back dark hair. He walked behind her, carrying himself like a bodyguard. Courtney paused at the opening to the living room, her gaze roving over it and finally setting on Sabina. She groaned inwardly as Jonathan's lover made her way over.

Todd and Julie appeared from the kitchen. Courtney flicked a glance at them before turning to look Sabina right in the eye. "I'm sorry that I wasn't here today. I just didn't think I had it in me. But I wanted to let you know that I'll be moving out of the house, and I'll try to do it as fast as possible."

Against her better judgment, Sabina asked about the baby. "I know Marisa is very worried that she's not going to see the child, who'll be her little brother or sister."

Courtney looked nervously back at the guy who hovered near the foyer, too far back to hear their conversation. "I'm working with an agency that's found a family who'd like to adopt the baby. I made the arrangements so that Marisa can be allowed full contact with her brother. In the meantime, I'm telling people I'm a surrogate."

Julie wrinkled her forehead. "You do know that's illegal in New York State, right?"

Courtney shrugged. "Nobody's questioned me on it. Anyway, I just wanted to tell you about the house."

"Thank you," Sabina replied. "Is there anything you'd like of Jonathan's?"

Courtney looked down at her left hand. Had she already hocked the ring Jonathan had given her? "I don't think so. I'll just collect some of my things and be gone. I'll let Marisa know when I'm fully moved out."

"Okay."

Sabina watched as Courtney turned around, walking up next to the tall, dark, and oddly creepy guy hovering in the background. He put his hand on her back possessively, and Sabina didn't doubt Courtney had found a new man to take care of her. When Courtney said she told people she was a surrogate, what she meant was that she told the guy she was carrying someone else's baby to explain her pregnancy.

They watched as the two ascended the stairs. Julie moved to stand beside Sabina.

"I guess that solves the problem," she scoffed. "What's with the guy she's with?"

Todd laughed. "I didn't know sugar daddies came that young."

Sabina shrugged. "Honestly, it's all the better for me. I don't have to evict her. I don't have to fight with her. She's leaving on her own accord. It is sad though; she was the only one of the multiple women that Jonathan cheated on me with who was actually capable of breaking up our marriage. It's rather sad how she suckered him in. Even so, I don't know whether to be angry with her or thank her for setting me free."

"I would definitely go with thanks," Julie said. "Does Hallmark make cards for that?"

Sabina smiled. "Maybe they ought to."

Julie looked at her watch. "Let's finish up. You guys want to come back to my house for some Chinese or something?"

"You aren't offering to cook?" Todd asked.

Julie glared at him.

"I'm game," Sabina said.

"If you'll let me," Todd said timidly.

"What about Marisa?" Julie asked.

"I'll go find her," Todd volunteered and headed for the stairs.

"Do you think she'll want to come?" Julie asked.

"If she wants to eat tonight, she will," Sabina said.

Courtney and her friend came down the stairs. She carried several blouses and sweaters hung on the expensive wooden hangers Jonathan had ordered for his suits, while her mystery man handled a jumbo-sized suitcase Sabina didn't recognize. She wasn't going to quibble about the hangers. She just wanted the little homewrecker out of her house!

"When I've finished cleaning out my things, I'll leave the keys to the house on the entry table and lock the door," Courtney promised.

"Thank you," Sabina said.

They watched as the couple left the house.

"You going to change the locks as soon as the door closes behind her?" Julie asked.

"You better believe it. And change the code on the garage door opener—even if she leaves hers."

Julie looked around the room. "So, you'll be back to being a homeowner again. When do you think you'll move back in?"

Sabina shrugged. "It can't happen until after I undo all the damage Courtney's inflicted. But it occurs to me that Missy and I might celebrate Christmas here. I think she'd like that. Then again, it might just reinforce Jonathan's absence. We'll have to talk about it. I still have three months left on my sublet."

"But it's not nearly as comfortable!" Julie protested.

Sabina offered a sardonic smile. "And it doesn't hold any bad memories, either." Plus, it was there that she'd first made love with Steve.

She'd told him about Jonathan's service and the reception, but unlike Courtney, she wasn't willing to parade her new man around when Jonathan had been dead less than a week. *If* Steve was to *be* her man. It was awkward to try to date someone when you'd only officially been a widow for a few days. And, of course, she had Marisa's fragile state of mind to consider.

"I'm not in a hurry," Steve told her. "You're worth waiting for."

Marisa and Todd came down the stairs, with Missy in the lead. "Chinese food?" she asked sounding hopeful.

"Put in your order now," Julie said, "I'm going to call it in and pick it up on the way."

"Chicken egg foo yung for me, please."

"Hey, that's my favorite!" Todd said, grinning.

Sabina glared at him.

"I mean, yeah, it's okay."

"I'd be satisfied with an eggroll and some hot and sour soup," Sabina piped up.

"I'll order at least a quart," Julie promised.

"Okay, then we rendezvous at your place in...?"

"Half an hour," Julie said.

"Sounds good to me," Sabina agreed.

Julie whipped out her phone and headed for the foyer and the coat closet.

"Shall we go in one car or two?" Todd asked.

"One," Sabina said. "We'll take my car and then we can drop you off here to pick up yours on the way back. That is if you don't mind sticking around to wait for us after we eat."

Todd shot a besotted look in Marisa's direction. "Sure, why not?"

Luckily the girl's attention was on her phone.

"Fine. You won't mind sitting in the back seat, will you?" Sabina asked.

"Alone?"

"Todd!" Sabina warned.

"No. Not at all."

In some ways, Sabina would be glad when Marisa returned to college, but for now...she'd just enjoy the peace that seemed to have settled over them. After all, with Jonathan gone, they were all each other had.

"Fine."

They heard the door close.

"We should bring dessert," Marisa said.

"We can stop at the grocery store and pick up a cake or some-thing," Sabina said. "We'd better get going if we want to arrive while the food's still hot."

The three of them headed for the entryway closet to retrieve their coats.

"Dibs for riding shotgun," Marisa said as she headed out the door. Hadn't she heard a word they'd said in the past few minutes?

Todd followed Marisa, but Sabina hung back for a moment, taking a look at the house that would soon be her home once again. She'd once loved that house, but not anymore.

She turned off the last of the lights and closed the door. In doing so, she closed a chapter of her life.

EPILOGUE

One Year Later

$\mathcal{A}$lthough the sun had set more than an hour before, Sabina sat at her desk and looked down at the list before her. "I need you to order the fabrics for the Charleston account draperies. And make sure to remind them to package it correctly this time. Last time, it was a total disaster."

Todd sat across from Sabina in her freshly decorated office in the same location she launched her business just fourteen months before. "Got it. And what about the sentencing next week?"

Sabina flipped through her calendar. "You know I'll be there for that. Any chance to see Charles Patterson go down for what he did to his clients is something I would reschedule my death for."

Todd laughed loudly, shaking his head. "Seeing the look on his face when you walk in and see him in that trendy orange jumpsuit will be sublime."

Sabina giggled. "I don't think he'll be in a jumpsuit, but I'd pay money to see that, too."

Todd shook his head closing his notebook. "It was bad enough that he stole all that money from those clients, but then to be charged with tax evasion on ten million bucks, make a run for it, and get caught trying to cross the Mexican border... I can't tell you how excited I was to see that picture of him handcuffed on the ground."

Sabina raised a hand to her mouth, trying not to laugh too loudly. "And he was wearing that dreadful purple ascot. Who dresses like that when they're about to skip the country to avoid prison?"

They laughed, not feeling a bit sorry. Charles Patterson had finally gotten what was coming to him, and every client he left behind seemed to be heading straight to Sabina Reigns Designs to redecorate their homes. In fact, her schedule was so full that she was booked solid for nearly a year with a waiting list of potential clients to boot. Her business was thriving and Sabina was more than ready to tackle even more ambitious projects to grow her firm. The local paper's two-page article on the Parkview Manor project hadn't hurt, either, spreading the word about her business. She'd had to hire two clerks to handle the walk-in trade and was about to hire another associate to help juggle and implement the work that was pending.

"What are you two laughing about?" a smiling Steve asked. He stood at the office entrance.

Sabina's heart did that little jump it always did when she saw her guy.

"The demise of our arch-nemesis. What have you got in those bags? It smells great," Todd said and stood.

Steve held them up, looking smug. "Tikka masala, garlic naan, and samosas. I hit the Indian takeout because I figured you guys would be here late—*again*."

Todd scoffed. "Just because we're a little late planning our first-anniversary party doesn't mean we aren't going to do it."

"You keep saying that, but I never hear about the details. Like a date."

Sabina pointed at Todd. "You're the one who decided it was important."

"It is and I stand by my choice even if I'll look like a zombie when it happens." Todd stood. "I assume that since you got in here without us knowing it, that we forgot to lock the showroom door—again."

"You got it."

Todd headed for the showroom.

Sabina laughed as she stood up and walked around the desk, leaning up and giving Steve what she hoped was a satisfying kiss. "It's always good to see you—but better when you bring food."

Steve grinned as he unpacked the bags and searched for serving utensils.

Sabina couldn't help but think back to a year before when there seemed to be nothing but stumbling blocks when it came to dating Steve. The night after Jonathan's funeral, he'd shown up at her apartment with a bottle of sake and five different kinds of sushi. They'd spent the evening talking and laughing, forgetting about all the drama that had occurred. From that day on, Steve became a priority in Sabina's life.

Marisa pushed back at it at first, as Sabina knew she would, but after about six months of Steve always being there when she came home from college to see her baby brother, Matthew, she started to come around. No one could replace Jonathan in her life, but at least she was no longer resentful of the relationship, and she wasn't giving Steve the stink eye every time she thought he wasn't looking, either.

Sabina had been apprehensive about Marisa and the adoptive family, hoping her daughter didn't get hurt in the process. But the family had kept their word and seemed to like Marisa, so she got to see her little brother as often as she liked. To Sabina's surprise, dealing with the situation had given Marisa a new maturity and she seemed to better appreciate how charmed a life she'd led. Even Sabina couldn't resist the little guy's chubby cheeks. He was the spitting image of Jonathan, and after the anger had faded and she was exactly where she wanted it to be, she no longer resented her dead husband. Surprisingly, she didn't think about him much at all, which was rather sad.

"Are we seeing Julie and Zoey this weekend?" Steve asked, doling out rice, chicken, and placing a half slice of naan on each plate.

Sabina took hers and moved to the quaint bistro table they'd recently installed in the kitchen. "I think Julie's taking Zoey to a concert. Some band that Zoey's been wanting to see."

Steve nodded. "I'm just glad they're getting along and seem to have moved beyond all that bickering."

"They've had their moments over the last year, and they still have a lot to work through, but I think because they invested in therapy, they're both a lot happier. Once Zoey started dealing with losing Robin, she was able to open her heart back up to her mother. And Julie had to remind herself just how much she loved her daughter." Sabina let out a breath. "I know firsthand how hard *that* can be."

Steve leaned over and gave Sabina a kiss on the cheek. "But you're perfect."

Sabina rolled her eyes. "I like how you suck up to me. You should continue to do that."

Steve laughed. "I can *definitely* do that." He put a hand to his mouth and called, "Hey, Todd, get in here before we eat your share."

"Coming!"

The three of them sat and ate. Todd and Steve talked sports and Sabina paused to gaze at the two new men in her life. She still tended to watch Todd like a hawk when Marisa was around, but she couldn't have asked for a better assistant. And her relationship with Steve grew stronger every day. The fact that Marisa and David got along so well didn't hurt, either. And while Sabina and Steve decided that they weren't ready to move in together, they were dedicated to each other on a level deeper than Sabina had thought she was capable of.

"Hey, 'bina, did the realtor finally get your listing up?" Steve asked, pulling Sabina from her reflective thoughts.

"Yes, she did," Sabina replied and took a bite of bread. "It went live yesterday, and there's going to be an open house next week. I think I've done pretty much everything I can to ensure the house sells fast."

"It's gorgeous," Todd pronounced. "I predict a bidding war."

"From your lips to God's ears," Sabina said and laughed.

"Is Marisa finally getting over the fact you're letting it go?" Steve asked before digging into his sauce and rice.

Sabina shrugged. "I think so. The last time she was here we had a long talk. I think she finally understands that I have to move on. That no matter how many coats of paint or changes of furniture I put in that house, it would always be a constant reminder of the past. Besides, the bungalow I found here in Pittsford is a clean slate and I can't wait to get started putting my own stamp on it."

Steve nodded. "That reminds me. I need to price the materials for the kitchen reno. And that master bathroom..." He shuddered and Sabina and Todd laughed.

Sabina swallowed a bite of spicy chicken and reached into the pocket of her slacks. "That reminds me. I made you a key for the new house so you can take measurements and start work whenever you can schedule it. I'm thinking about going ahead and moving into it as soon as possible."

"Are you sure you want to live in a work zone?" Steve asked.

"We'll soon find out."

Steve's phone rang. He pulled it from the clip on his belt,

looking at the number. "I'm sorry, I'm going to step outside. It's one of my clients. He likes to talk—and boy can he."

Sabina giggled and nodded. As soon as he left, Todd grabbed the last piece of bread. "You didn't want this did you?"

She shook her head and placed her fork on the plate before she sat back with a smile. Everything seemed to have come full circle. Her business was booming, she would soon move to a new-to-her house, she had a steady beau, and her relationship with her daughter continued to improve.

Todd tapped her on the arm. "Wanna talk about the wine for the party?"

Sabina groaned. "Not after eating spicy food. I think I'm done for the day. And you should be, too!"

"Yes, ma'am. But I just *love* working here," Todd said and mopped up the last of the sauce on his plate. He got up, taking his dish and cutlery to the sink to rinse.

Sabina looked around, taking in the showroom beyond, her office with shelves on the walls, beautiful pictures, and an attractive French antique desk that never failed to welcome her. She smiled to herself and thought, *When life gives you lemons, you pick the seeds, plant them, nurture them, and grow your own damn lemon trees.*

And that was exactly what Sabina had done.

ABOUT LORRAINE BARTLETT

The immensely popular Booktown Mystery series is what put Lorraine Bartlett's pen name Lorna Barrett on the New York Times Bestseller list, but it's her talent--whether writing as Lorna, or L.L. Bartlett, or Lorraine Bartlett—that keeps her in the hearts of her readers. This multi-published, Agatha-nominated author pens the exciting Jeff Resnick Mysteries as well as the acclaimed Victoria Square Mystery series, the Tales of Telenia adventure-fantasy saga, and now the Lotus Bay Mysteries, and has many short stories and novellas to her name(s). Check out the descriptions and links to all her works, and sign up for her emailed newsletter on her website.

Not familiar with all of Lorraine's work? Check out **A Cozy Mystery Sampler,** which is FREE for all ebook formats.

If you enjoyed *SABINA REIGNS*, please consider reviewing it on your favorite online review site. Thank you!

Find Lorraine on Social Media
www.LorraineBartlett.com

ALSO BY LORRAINE BARTLETT

THE LOTUS BAY MYSTERIES

Panty Raid (A Tori Cannon-Kathy Grant mini mystery)

With Baited Breath

Christmas At Swans Nest

A Reel Catch

The Best From Swans Nest (A Lotus Bay Cookbook)

THE VICTORIA SQUARE MYSTERIES

A Crafty Killing

The Walled Flower

One Hot Murder

Dead, Bath and Beyond (with Laurie Cass)

Yule Be Dead (with Gayle Leeson)

Murder Ink (with Gayle Leeson)

A Murderous Misconception (with Gayle Lesson)

Dead Man's Hand (with Gayle Leeson)

Recipes To Die For: A Victoria Square Cookbook

LIFE ON VICTORIA SQUARE

Carving Out A Path

A Basket Full of Bargains

The Broken Teacup

It's Tutu Much

The Reluctant Bride

Tea'd Off

Life On Victoria Square Vol. 1

A Look Back

Room At The Inn

Cheated By Death

Bound By Suggestion

Dark Waters

Shattered Spirits

JEFF RESNICK'S PERSONAL FILES

Evolution: Jeff Resnick's Backstory

A Jeff Resnick Six Pack

When The Spirit Moves You

Bah! Humbug

Cold Case

Spooked!

Crybaby

Eyewitness

A Part of The Pattern

Abused: A Daughter's Story

Off Script

Writing as Lorna Barrett

THE BOOKTOWN MYSTERIES

Murder Is Binding

Bookmarked For Death

Bookplate Special

Chapter & Hearse

Sentenced To Death

Murder On The Half Shelf

Not The Killing Type

Book Clubbed

A Fatal Chapter

Title Wave

A Just Clause

Poisoned Pages

A Killer Edition

Handbook For Homicide

WITH THE COZY CHICKS

The Cozy Chicks Kitchen

Tea Time With The Cozy Chicks

Made in the USA
Middletown, DE
13 July 2021